NO-GRID SURVIVAL GUIDE

Emergency Preparedness When The Grid Goes Down

Master the Essential Skills and Strategies to Safeguard Your Family, Build Self-Sufficiency, and Thrive in Crisis

DENNIS CARSON

CONTENTS

Chapter Nine

Home Security and Protection 110

Chapter Ten

Thriving in Long-Term Power Outage 117

Chapter Eleven

Financial Preparedness 124

Chapter Twelve

Your Grid Down Preparedness Journey   130

Resources 133

CHAPTER ONE

INTRODUCTION

Preparedness is the ultimate confidence
builder.

Vince Lombardi

Imagine being stuck in your home for days without power, water, or heat during a winter storm. How would you cope with the freezing temperatures, the lack of communication, and the stress of not knowing when things will get better? This is what happened to millions of people in Texas in February 2021, when a series of severe winter storms caused widespread blackouts and water shortages. In a desperate bid to fend off the biting cold, some people resorted to burning their own furniture, while others faced life-threatening water shortages and health issues. Countless families and communities found themselves unprepared for such a disaster, and as a result, suffered greatly.

But it doesn't have to be this way. When it comes to no-grid survival, knowledge is your greatest ally. By understanding the potential causes and consequences of power outages, you can arm yourself with the skills to safeguard your family and thrive in a world without electricity. In this chapter, we'll explore the various scenarios that could lead to grid failure, why it's crucial to be prepared, and how to take the first steps toward self-sufficiency and resilience.

When Darkness Falls

Picture this: one moment you're going about your daily life, and the next, you're plunged into an unnerving darkness that stretches as far as the eye can see. In the event of a power grid failure, widespread power loss disrupts society's vital functions, leaving countless people stranded without essentials like clean water, food, and communication.

The U.S. Energy Information Administration (2022) reports that the average American faced over 7 hours of power outages in 2021, and though these brief intermissions may seem bearable, a long-term grid failure could have serious consequences for our life.

The notion of a widespread power grid failure might seem like a tale ripped from the pages of a dystopian novel, but history has shown that such events have indeed occurred in North America, urging us to be prepared for the worst.

Remember the 2003 Northeast Blackout? It cast fifty million people into darkness for four days, racking up economic losses of up to $10 billion. And equally chilling is the 2013 incident that unfolded just south of San Jose, marking the most serious assault on power grid in history. For a tense twenty minutes, unidentified gunmen ruthlessly targeted high voltage transformers at the Metcalf Power substation, damaging 17 of the 21 massive transformers and vanishing without a trace. Had they succeeded in their sinister mission, the entirety of Silicon Valley could have been brought to its knees (Whitaker, 2022).

As if these real-life events weren't enough, the National Geographic Channel's series, "American Blackout," lays bare the terrifying reality of a long-term electrical grid failure. Fast-forward to 2022, and the threat hasn't subsided, with 107 physical attacks on the U.S. electrical grid, some linked to domestic extremists plotting coordinated strikes (O'Connor & Jamali, 2023).

But the danger doesn't end there. Our electrical grid remains susceptible to disruptions from a myriad of sources, including extreme weather, cyberattacks, and even the sun. That's right – the sun itself can unleash solar flares capable of frying our electronics and transformers, leading to extensive blackouts. In fact, this almost happened in 2012, when a massive solar storm narrowly missed Earth by a week.

Identifying Potential Causes

There are several potential causes of power outages, and understanding them is the first step toward effective preparedness. Some of the most common causes include:

Natural disasters: Events like hurricanes, earthquakes, and solar storms can damage power lines, substations, and other infrastructure. The Associated Press (2022) has analyzed government data and found that power outages due to severe weather have doubled over the past two decades in the US.

Electromagnetic Pulse (EMP) Attacks: EMPs are bursts of electromagnetic radiation that can result from natural events like solar flares or human-made causes such as a high-altitude nuclear detonation. An EMP attack can cause huge damage to electrical systems and infrastructure, including power grids.

Cyberattacks: As our world becomes more interconnected, the risk of cyberattacks on our power grid increases. A successful attack on the grid could result in widespread power outages. In 2015, a cyberattack in Ukraine left over 200,000 people without electricity, highlighting the vulnerability of modern power systems.

Terrorism or sabotage: Deliberate acts of destruction, such as bombing or vandalism, can also lead to grid failure. While these events are relatively rare, the potential consequences can be catastrophic.

System failures or human error: Accidents, equipment malfunctions, and human errors can also cause grid disruptions. In 2003, a massive blackout in the United States and Canada affected over 50 million people, primarily due to a software bug and inadequate communication between power companies.

Taking Control of Your Destiny

It's easy to underestimate the value of preparedness or dismiss the concept as the domain of doomsday preppers. Yet, the truth is that being prepared isn't just for the fanatics. It's an essential practice that can make a world of difference in the face of unexpected disasters.

Imagine two neighbors, Just-in-Time John and Plan-Ahead Jane, living in the same community. John has always been skeptical, insisting that the odds of a significant grid down event occurring in his lifetime are slim to none. He believes that even if such an event were to happen, the government would step in and provide all the necessary support. Jane, on the other hand, has taken time and effort in learning the ins and outs of emergency preparedness.

She has stocked up on essentials like food, water, and alternative power sources, and her family has a well-rehearsed plan in place.

When an unexpected disaster strikes, rendering the power grid inoperable, John's family is left scrambling in the dark, without access to basic necessities. In contrast, Jane's family is better equipped to cope with the challenges, thanks to their foresight and planning. This simple example illustrates the immense value of preparedness in times of crisis.

Being prepared is about more than just stocking up on supplies or learning survival skills, though these are important. It's about cultivating a mindset of self-reliance, empowering you to take control of your destiny. You don't need to build a bunker or amass a decade's worth of supplies to make a difference. Even small, incremental steps can add up over time, enhancing your overall readiness and resilience.

So, why wait for disaster to strike before taking action? Embrace the mindset of preparedness today. As the adage says, "An ounce of prevention is worth a pound of cure." In the uncertain world we live in, there's never been a better time to take control of your destiny and arm yourself with the knowledge and skills needed to face whatever challenges may come your way.

Key Takeaways

Grid down scenarios can be caused by various factors, including natural disasters, cyberattacks, terrorism, and system failures. Understanding these causes is the first step toward effective preparedness.

Being prepared is crucial for ensuring the safety, health, and well-being of your family during times of crisis. It also contributes to building resilience and self-sufficiency in the face of adversity.

Everyone can learn the skills and be prepared – all it takes is a little determination, dedication, and the right guidance.

Remember, the journey toward grid down preparedness is a rewarding and empowering experience. With the right mindset, you can overcome any challenge and protect your loved ones in times of uncertainty.

In the next chapter, we'll explore the critical components of a foolproof emergency plan, including establishing priorities, identifying vulnerabilities, and creating actionable steps. Get ready to embark on a journey that will transform the way you think about preparedness and empower you to thrive in an unpredictable world.

References:

Energy Information Administration. (2022, November 14). U.S. electricity customers averaged seven hours of power interruptions in 2021. Today in Energy. Retrieved from https://www.eia.gov/todayinenergy/detail.php?id=54639

Whitaker, B. (2022, August 28). Vulnerable U.S. electric grid facing threats from Russia and domestic terrorists. CBS News. Retrieved from https://www.cbsnews.com/news/america-electric-grid-60-minutes-2022-08-28/

O'Connor, T., & Jamali, N. (2023, January 11). Domestic terrorists could take out U.S. power grid—and attacks have started. Newsweek. Retrieved from https://www.newsweek.com/2023/01/20/domestic-terrorists-could-take-out-us-power-grid-attacks-have-started-1772786.html

Associated Press. (2022, April 6). US power outages from severe weather have doubled in 20 years. The Guardian. Retrieved from https://www.theguardian.com/us-news/2022/apr/06/us-power-outages-severe-weather-doubled-in-20-years

Chapter Two

CRAFTING YOUR EMERGENCY BLUEPRINT

In preparing for battle, I have always found
that plans are useless, but planning is
indispensable.

Dwight D. Eisenhower

To protect yourself and your family from the unpredictable power outages, it's crucial to have a solid blueprint that serves as the guiding light in times of darkness. In this chapter, we'll discuss the process of crafting a family emergency plan, tailored specifically to meet the challenges of power outages.

Building the Framework

Below are the key components necessary for building a robust plan to help your family weather the storm of a prolonged power outage:

Identifying Potential Risks

The first step in designing an emergency plan is to identify the potential risks specific to your area. Natural disasters such as hurricanes, tornadoes, earthquakes, and floods, as well as man-made hazards like industrial accidents, should be considered. Research your local area's history, consult local authorities, and use resources like Federal Emergency Management Agency (FEMA) website to gain a better understanding of the risks your family may face.

Emergency Contact Information

During a power outage, communication channels may be disrupted. Gather important phone numbers, including family members, friends, neighbors, and emergency services, so that your family can stay connected and informed.

Evacuation Routes and Meeting Points

Power outages can be accompanied by other emergencies, such as fires. Determine the safest evacuation routes from your home and identify predetermined meeting points in case family members are separated during an emergency.

Communication Strategies

Establish a communication plan that outlines how your family will stay connected during a power outage. Consider backup ways to communicate if traditional channels are unavailable, such as:

- Battery-powered or hand-crank radios for receiving emergency broadcasts

- Walkie-talkies or satellite phones for direct communication with family members

- Social media or messaging apps that can operate on limited connectivity

Alternative Light and Heat Sources

Extended power outages can leave your home without light and heat, making it difficult to carry out daily tasks and stay warm. Plan for alternative light and heat sources, such as:

- Battery-operated or solar-powered lanterns and flashlights

- Candles and matches or lighters

- Propane or kerosene heaters (with proper ventilation)

- Warm clothing and blankets

Food and Water Supply Management

During a power outage, access to fresh food and water might be limited. Plan for maintaining a safe food and water supply:

- Stock up on non-perishable food items that don't need cooking or refrigeration

- Store at least a 72-hour supply of water for each family member

- Learn how to safely store perishable food during a power outage, such as using coolers and ice packs

Medical Needs and Essential Supplies

Account for the specific medical needs of your family members and ensure that your emergency kit contains necessary medication, first aid supplies, and other essentials. Keep in mind that some medical equipment may require backup power sources, such as portable generators or battery backups.

Pets and Animals

Include plans for pets and animals, such as pet-friendly shelters, and emergency supplies. Power outages may affect their well-being, and having a plan in place will help ensure their safety.

Important Documents

Keep copies of essential documents, such as birth certificates, passports, insurance policies, and property deeds, in a secure and easily accessible location. During a power outage, electronic access to these documents may be limited, so having physical copies on hand is crucial.

Financial Preparedness

During a power outage, access to financial services may be limited or disrupted. To ensure your family's financial well-being during an emergency, consider the following steps:

- Keep a reasonable amount of cash on hand in small denominations, as ATMs and electronic payment systems may not be operational during a power outage.

- Review your insurance policies to make sure you have coverage for potential damages caused by power outages or related events.

- Develop a post-emergency financial recovery plan to help your family get back on track after a power outage. This may include strategies for replenishing your emergency savings, and addressing property damages.

Bringing It to Life

We discussed the key components of a family emergency plan. Now, it's time to bring that plan to life. In this section, we'll explore the steps to make your plan more effective, including engaging family members, customizing the plan, building a support network, and practicing the plan regularly.

Engaging Family Members

Discuss the plan openly, addressing individual concerns and ensuring everyone understands their responsibilities during a power outage. By engaging everyone, you'll foster a strong sense of teamwork and unity, which is essential during a crisis.

Customizing Your Plan

Every family is unique, and so should be their emergency plan. Adapt your plan to cater to the specific needs of your family members. Consider medical conditions, dietary restrictions, ages, and abilities when designing your plan.

Building a Support Network

Share your plan with neighbors, friends, and relatives to create a community-based support system. By doing so, you can rely on each other for help during emergencies. Discuss your plans with your support network and identify areas where you can work together, such as sharing resources, skills, or shelter.

Practicing the Plan

Regular drills are essential for ensuring your family is well-prepared. Practice evacuation routes, test communication strategies, and familiarize your family with the location and use of emergency supplies.

Staying Informed

Keeping up-to-date with local emergency information is crucial for adjusting your plan accordingly. Sign up for local alert systems, follow news updates, and be aware of any changes to your community's emergency management policies.

Adapting to Change

Your family's situation and the risks you face may change over time, so it's important to keep your plan up-to-date. Regularly review your plan, taking into account new family members, changes in medical conditions, or shifts in your local environment.

Key Takeaways

During power outages, a comprehensive plan helps ensure proper communication, healthcare management, and resource rationing.

Taking small, incremental steps towards preparedness can make a significant difference during a crisis.

Engage all family members in the planning process to foster a sense of teamwork and unity.

Customize your plan to cater to the specific needs and circumstances of your family members.

Build a support network with neighbors, friends, and relatives to create a community-based system during power outages.

Conduct regular drills to reinforce the plan's details and improve overall preparedness.

Adapt your plan to any changes in your family's situation or the risks you face, ensuring it remains relevant and effective.

In the next chapter, we will explore emergency power solutions. This will include backup power options and strategies to ensure you have the resources to navigate a power outage effectively.

CHAPTER THREE

EMERGENCY POWER SOLUTIONS

Energy is the golden thread that connects economic growth, social equity, and environmental sustainability.

Ban Ki-moon

This chapter will look at different emergency power solutions. Each solution has its own pros and cons, making them suitable for different needs. We'll also talk about saving energy and using it efficiently, as these are key in managing power. With the information provided in this chapter, you will be better equipped to decide which power solution is most suitable for your needs and how to implement it effectively.

Lighting Solutions

Battery-Powered LED Lights and Lanterns

Battery-powered LED lights and lanterns are an energy-efficient and portable option. They are available in various sizes and styles, including flashlights, headlamps, lanterns, and even string lights. These LED lights often have adjustable brightness settings and can last for hours on a single set of batteries. To ensure you have adequate lighting, stock up on batteries and consider having a mix of LED lighting options to suit different needs and spaces.

Solar-Powered Lighting Options

Solar lanterns: These are portable and rechargeable, usually with built-in panels that charge in daylight and light up at night. They often have multiple brightness settings and may also feature USB ports for charging small devices.

Solar-powered outdoor lights: These lights are designed for use in gardens, walkways, or around the perimeter of your property. They often have motion sensors and automatically turn on when it gets dark.

Indoor solar lights: Some solar-powered lights are designed for indoor use, with separate solar panels that can be placed out-side to charge during the day. These lights may have a variety of mounting options, such as hanging or tabletop placement.

Oil Lamps, Candles, and Other Options

Oil lamps: These lamps use a wick and fuel like lamp oil or kerosene to give continuous light. They come in various styles, including traditional glass lamps and more modern metal designs. Be sure to store an adequate supply of fuel and wicks for extended use.

Candles: Candles are a simple lighting solution, but they burn relatively quickly and require close supervision. Stock up on long-lasting candles and use sturdy candleholders to minimize fire risks.

Glow sticks: These are safe, non-toxic sticks that light up for temporary lighting when activated. They are waterproof, non-toxic, and do not produce heat or flames, making them a safe option for emergencies.

Safety Considerations and Tips for Using Alternative Lighting Sources

When using alternative lighting sources, keep the following safety tips in mind:

Ensure proper ventilation: When using oil lamps or candles, ensure there is adequate ventilation to prevent the build-up of toxic fumes or smoke.

Keep flammable materials away: Place oil lamps, candles, and other open flame sources away from flammable materials, such as curtains, bedding, or furniture.

Use stable surfaces: Place lighting sources on stable, level surfaces to reduce the risk of accidents or spills.

Monitor children and pets: Keep a close eye on children and pets when using alternative lighting sources, as they may be attracted to the flame or light.

Store fuel and batteries safely: Keep fuel for oil lamps and spare batteries in a cool, dry place, away from heat sources or direct sunlight.

Be prepared to extinguish fires: Have fire extinguishers or other fire-fighting equipment readily available in case of an emergency.

Portable Generators

Portable generators are popular for their ease of movement, low cost, and simplicity. These generators come in various fuel types, each with its unique features. This section will discuss gas, diesel, propane, and dual-fuel portable generators, their pros and cons, maintenance and safety tips, as well as sizing and power output considerations.

Types of portable generators

Gasoline generators: Gasoline generators are common because they're widely available and usually cheaper. They are easy to start and can provide sufficient power for essential household needs.

Pros:

- Readily available fuel

- Lightweight and portable

- Lower initial cost

Cons:

- Shorter runtime (typically 8-12 hours per tank)

- Fuel storage can be hazardous

- Less fuel-efficient compared to diesel generators

- May not work well in extreme temperatures

Diesel generators: Known for their fuel efficiency and durability, these generators tend to have a longer runtime and require less maintenance compared to gasoline generators. However, they are often heavier and more expensive.

Pros:

- Longer runtime (typically 12-24 hours per tank)

- Fuel-efficient

- Durable and longer-lasting engine

Cons:

- Higher initial cost

- Heavier and less portable

- Diesel fuel can be more difficult to store

- May not work well in extremely cold temperatures

Propane generators: Propane generators have gained popularity due to their clean-burning nature and extended shelf life of fuel. They emit fewer pollutants compared to gasoline and diesel generators and can be stored for long periods without degrading.

Pros:

- Clean-burning fuel with fewer emissions

- Longer shelf-life for fuel storage

- Quieter operation

Cons:

- Less energy-dense fuel, which can result in shorter runtime (typically 8-12 hours per tank)

- Heavier propane tanks can be cumbersome

- May not work well in extremely cold temperatures

Dual-fuel generators: Dual-fuel generators offer versatility by allowing the user to switch between two fuel types, typically gasoline and propane. This provides flexibility in fuel availability and allows for extended runtime by utilizing both fuel sources.

Pros:

- Fuel flexibility

- Can switch fuel sources to extend runtime

- Offers benefits of both gasoline and propane generators

Cons:

- Higher initial cost

- More complex systems may require additional maintenance

Proper sizing and power output

When choosing a portable generator, it is crucial to consider the size and power output required for your specific needs. To determine the appropriate generator size, create a list of essential appliances and devices you plan to power during a grid down situation. Add up the total wattage of these items to estimate your power requirements.

It's crucial to remember that refrigerators and air conditioners have a higher starting wattage than running wattage. Make sure to account for this when calculating your power needs.

When selecting a generator, choose one with a power output slightly higher than your estimated wattage requirements to account for any unforeseen power needs and avoid overloading the generator. By considering your specific power requirements and weighing the pros and cons of each portable generator type, you can choose the best solution for your needs.

Other considerations

When considering a portable generator, keep the following factors in mind:

Fuel availability and storage: Ensure you have a reliable fuel source and the ability to store it safely.

Runtime: Consider how long you expect to rely on the generator and whether refueling will be feasible.

Noise level: Some generators can be quite loud, which might be a concern in your areas or if you're trying to maintain a low profile.

Portability and size: Evaluate whether you'll need to move the generator and if you have space to store it.

Maintenance and reliability: Research the generator's maintenance requirements and reliability, as well as the availability of replacement parts.

Working temperature: Make sure the generator you choose can operate effectively in the temperature extremes you may experience in your area.

Generator maintenance and safety tips

Regularly inspect your generator to ensure optimal performance and longevity. This includes checking oil levels, air filters, and spark plugs.

Always use your generator outdoors in a well-ventilated area, away from doors and windows, to avoid carbon monoxide poisoning.

Store fuel safely in properly labeled containers, away from heat sources and living spaces.

Use an extension cord rated for outdoor use and the wattage of your generator.

Do not overload your generator by trying to power too many appliances at once. Prioritize essential items and stagger usage.

Turn off your generator and allow it to cool before refueling to avoid potential fire hazards.

Portable generators provide a reliable and convenient source of emergency power during a power outage. By understanding the differences between gasoline, diesel, propane, and dual-fuel generators, as well as their pros and cons, you can decide on the best generator type for your situation. Regular maintenance and adherence to safety guidelines are crucial to ensure the safe and efficient operation of your generator. Lastly, considering your power requirements and selecting an appropriately sized generator will help ensure that you have sufficient power to meet your essential needs. With careful planning and preparation, you can rely on a portable generator to help keep your home functioning when the power goes out.

Solar Power Solutions

Harnessing the sun's energy can provide electricity to power essential appliances and devices when the grid is down. In this section, we will explore different solar power solutions, battery storage options, and considerations when choosing and installing a solar power system.

Solar Panels and Photovoltaic Systems

Photovoltaic (PV) systems are complete setups that harness solar energy to generate electricity for your home. Solar panels, the primary components of PV systems, convert sunlight into electricity using photovoltaic cells. This electricity can be used to power your home or charge batteries for later use. Solar panels are usually mounted on rooftops or ground-mounted racks.

To select the right photovoltaic system for your needs, you should consider the following factors:

Types of Solar Panels: There are three main types: monocrystalline, polycrystalline, and thin-film. Monocrystalline panels are the most efficient and usually the most expensive. Polycrystalline panels have slightly lower efficiency but are more affordable. Thin-film panels are the least efficient and least expensive, suitable for those with limited space or budget.

Efficiency of Solar Panels: Solar panel efficiency is about how well they can convert sunlight into electricity. The higher the efficiency, the more electricity you get from the same size panel, but typically these panels cost more. So, when choosing, consider how much electricity you need and how much you're willing to spend.

Power output: Solar panels are rated by their power output, measured in watts (W). Consider your energy needs and choose panels with a power output that can meet those needs.

Size and space requirements: Ensure you have enough space on your rooftop or property for the solar panel system. Consider the size and weight of the panels and the available mounting options.

Durability and warranty: Look for panels with a long warranty (at least 20-25 years) and a good track record for durability.

High-quality panels will last longer and require less maintenance.

Installation costs: Consider the cost of installing the solar panel system, including labor, permits, and any necessary electrical upgrades.

Local regulations and incentives: Research local regulations regarding solar panel installations, and check for available incentives or rebates that can help offset the costs.

To select the right system for your needs, start by determining your energy requirements and the available space on your property. Research different types of panels and compare their efficiency, power output, size, durability, warranty, and costs. Don't forget to consider local regulations and incentives. By carefully evaluating these factors, you can choose a solar panel system that will provide reliable power and meet your energy needs effectively.

Solar Generators and Portable Solar Chargers

Solar generators are devices that utilize solar panels to charge built-in batteries, which can then be used to power devices and appliances. While many solar generators are designed to be portable and convenient for various uses, there are also larger, stationary systems intended for more permanent or industrial applications. Portable solar chargers are smaller, lightweight options designed to charge devices like cellphones, tablets, and laptops directly.

Solar generators and portable solar chargers are valuable tools, providing a renewable and versatile energy source. When selecting one for your needs, consider the following factors:

Capacity: Solar generators and chargers come in various capacities, measured in watt-hours (Wh) or ampere-hours (Ah). Consider your energy needs and the devices you plan to power, and choose a generator or charger with sufficient capacity.

Power output: Check the power output (measured in watts) of the generator or charger to ensure it can handle the power demands of your devices. Some generators offer multiple output options, such as USB ports, 12V DC ports, and AC outlets, providing greater flexibility in powering a range of devices.

Solar panel efficiency: The efficiency of the solar panel determines how quickly the generator or charger can convert sunlight into usable energy. Higher efficiency panels will recharge the battery faster, ensuring you have power when you need it.

Portability: Consider the size and weight of the generator or charger, especially if you plan to transport it frequently. Smaller, lightweight options may be more convenient but could have lower capacity and output.

Durability and weather resistance: Opt for a generator or charger with a rugged design and weather-resistant features, ensuring it can withstand the elements and continue to function in various conditions.

Charge controller: A high-quality charge controller is essential for protecting the battery from overcharging and ensuring efficient charging. Look for generators and chargers with built-in charge controllers that offer features like maximum power point tracking (MPPT) for optimal performance.

Additional features: Some solar generators and chargers offer extra features, such as built-in LED lights, multiple charging options, and expandability (the ability to connect additional solar panels or batteries). Evaluate which features are essential for your needs and select a generator or charger that meets those requirements.

By considering these factors, you can select the best option for your needs, providing a reliable source of renewable energy. These devices can help you stay connected, power essential appliances, and maintain your safety and comfort when the grid goes down.

Battery Storage Options

Battery storage allows you to store excess solar power when the sun isn't shining. There are several battery options available, with the most common being lead-acid and lithium-ion batteries. When selecting a battery for your solar power system, consider the following factors:

Type of battery: As mentioned, lead-acid batteries are less expensive but don't last as long and can't hold as much energy. On the other hand, lithium-ion batteries are pricier, but they last longer, can hold more energy, and are more efficient overall.

Capacity: When choosing a battery, ensure it has enough capacity to meet your solar power system's output. Think about your energy usage and select a battery that can handle your needs without frequent recharges.

Depth of discharge (DoD): The DoD is the percentage of a battery's energy that can be used before recharging is required. A higher DoD means more usable energy, so consider this when selecting a battery.

Cycle life: The number of times a battery can be charged and used before it doesn't hold as much power. A battery with a higher cycle life will last longer.

Temperature tolerance: Batteries can be sensitive to extreme temperatures. Ensure the battery you choose is suitable for the temperature ranges in your area.

Maintenance requirements: Lead-acid batteries typically require more maintenance, such as checking and refilling electrolyte levels, while lithium-ion batteries are generally maintenance-free. Consider the time and effort you're willing to put into maintaining your battery storage system.

Price and warranty: Compare the costs and warranties of different battery options to determine which offers the best value for your needs.

To select the right battery storage for your solar power system, start by determining your energy requirements and the specifications of your solar power system. Assess the available battery options, considering factors such as type, capacity, DoD, cycle life, temperature tolerance, maintenance requirements, price, and warranty. By evaluating these factors, you can choose a battery that will provide reliable power and complement your solar power system effectively.

Proper System Sizing and Installation Tips

When sizing and installing a solar power system, keep the following in mind:

Accurately calculate your energy needs: Overestimating or underestimating your energy requirements can lead to an inefficient and costly system.

Position solar panels for optimal sunlight exposure: To get the most out of your solar panels, you'll need to position them where they can soak up the most sun. In the Northern Hemisphere, aim the panels south; in the Southern Hemisphere, point them north. Also, tilt the panels at an angle that catches the most sunlight throughout the day.

Ensure proper ventilation: Make sure there's good airflow around solar panels and batteries to stop them from overheating and keep them working well.

Consider a professional installer: If solar power systems seem complex, a professional can make sure it's set up right for the best performance and safety.

By understanding the different solar power solutions, battery storage options, and factors to consider when choosing and installing a system, you can harness the sun's energy to provide reliable power, while also contributing to a more sustainable energy future.

Wind Power Solutions

Small-Scale Wind Turbines for Residential Use

Wind power is a reliable source of renewable energy that can be harnessed by wind turbines. These turbines turn wind into electricity, providing an alternative power source during a black-out. Small-scale wind turbines have different designs, including horizontal-axis and vertical-axis turbines. Horizontal-axis turbines are more common and typically more efficient, while vertical-axis turbines can capture wind from any direction and are often more visually appealing.

Choosing the Right Wind Turbine

Selecting the right wind turbine for your needs requires careful consideration of several factors:

Wind resource: Assess the wind resource in your area. You need consistent and strong wind for an effective wind turbine. You can consult wind resource maps or hire a professional to conduct a site assessment.

Turbine size and power output: Select a turbine whose power output matches your energy needs. Turbines are rated in watts or kilowatts, and a larger turbine will generally produce more power.

Efficiency: Look for turbines with a high efficiency rating. Wind turbine efficiency is about how well it turns wind into electricity.

Budget: Determine your budget for purchasing and installing a wind turbine. Keep in mind that while the initial investment can be substantial, the long-term savings on your electricity bills can offset the costs.

Local regulations and permits: Research local regulations and permitting requirements for installing a wind turbine on your property. Some areas may have restrictions on the size, height, or location of turbines.

Installation and Maintenance

Correct installation and regular maintenance are key to your turbine's best performance. Consider the following when installing and maintaining your turbine:

Site selection: Choose a site with few obstructions and high average wind speed.

Professional installation: Hire a professional installer with experience in wind turbine installations to ensure your system is set up correctly and safely.

Routine maintenance: Regularly inspect and maintain your turbine, including checking for corrosion, loose bolts, and wear on moving parts. Proper maintenance can extend the lifespan of your turbine and improve its efficiency.

Safety precautions: Follow safety guidelines and precautions when working. This includes turning off the turbine before performing maintenance and staying clear of moving parts.

Combining Wind and Solar Power for a Hybrid System

For steadier power during outages, think about using both wind and solar power in a hybrid system. This type of system takes advantage of the complementary nature of wind and solar resources – when the sun isn't shining, the wind is often blowing, and vice versa. By harnessing both wind and solar power, you can increase your system's overall efficiency and reduce reliance on a single energy source.

A hybrid system typically consists of solar panels, a wind turbine, a charge controller, batteries for storing energy, and an inverter to convert the generated electricity for use in your home. To design and install a hybrid system, consult with professionals experienced in both solar and wind power solutions.

Other wind solutions

Micro Wind Turbines: Micro wind turbines, smaller and

designed for low-wind or urban areas, can be mounted on rooftops, walls, or poles and can supplement your power supply during an outage. However, their energy output is lower than that of larger wind turbines.

Portable Wind Turbines: Portable wind turbines are compact, lightweight, and easy to transport. They can be set up temporarily to provide emergency power for small devices and appliances.

Wind-powered Water Pumps: While not a direct source of electricity, wind-powered water pumps can be useful for pumping water from wells or other sources. These systems use the energy of the wind to move water, providing a reliable water supply.

By carefully considering your energy needs, available resources, and local regulations, you can select the most suitable wind power solution for your home.

Hydroelectric Power Solutions

Micro-Hydroelectric Systems for Residential Use

Micro-hydroelectric systems are small-scale power generation solutions that use flowing water to create electricity. They can provide a reliable and sustainable power source for homes located near a suitable water source, such as a stream or river. Micro-hydro systems typically consist of a turbine, generator, and control equipment, and they can be customized to suit various power requirements.

Pros and Cons of Hydroelectric Energy

Pros:

- Renewable and sustainable: Hydroelectric energy is renewable and sustainable, as it relies on the natural water cycle.

• Continuous power generation: Unlike solar and wind power, which are intermittent, micro-hydro systems can provide continuous power generation as long as there is a steady flow of water.

• Low environmental impact: Micro-hydro systems have a relatively low environmental impact, particularly when compared to large-scale hydroelectric dams.

Cons:

• Limited availability: Micro-hydro systems need a steady water source, so they can only be set up in certain places.

• Seasonal variations: The amount of water can change with the seasons, affecting how much power the system can produce.

• Initial investment: Installing a micro-hydro system can be expensive, particularly if civil works are required to divert water to the turbine.

Selecting a Micro-Hydro System

To choose the right system for your needs, consider the following factors:

Water resource: Assess the water resource on your property, including flow rate and head (vertical drop). Getting an expert evaluation can provide accurate data on the potential power generation capacity of your site.

System size: Choose a system with a power output that meets your energy needs. Micro-hydro systems are typically rated in watts or kilowatts.

Efficiency: Look for systems with high efficiency ratings to maximize power generation from water resources.

Budget: Determine your budget for installing a micro-hydro system. Consider both upfront costs and potential long-term savings on your electricity bills.

Local regulations and permits: Check local rules and needed permits for micro-hydro installations. Some locations may have restrictions on water diversion or other aspects of the project.

Installation and Maintenance

The installation begins with identifying a suitable water source with adequate flow and head, which is crucial for energy generation. A system of intake, pipeline (penstock), turbine, and generator is then carefully installed. The water is channeled from the source to the turbine through the penstock, driving the turbine connected to a generator, thus producing electricity.

To ensure efficiency and longevity, regular maintenance is critical. This includes cleaning the intake and filters to prevent blockages that reduce water flow. Inspecting the penstock for leaks, checking turbines and generators for wear and tear, and ensuring electrical connections are secure are all part of ongoing care. Regular monitoring helps in identifying issues early and keeping the system running smoothly.

By focusing on these aspects, you can effectively harness renewable energy from a micro-hydroelectric system, providing a sustainable and reliable power source.

Energy Conservation and Efficiency

Reducing Energy Consumption

During a grid-down situation, it's crucial to reduce energy consumption to make the most of your available resources. Some strategies for minimizing energy use include:

Prioritize essential needs: Focus on powering the most critical devices and appliances, such as heating and communication equipment. Turn off non-essential devices and unplug them to avoid standby power use.

Limit the use of high-energy appliances: Minimize the use of appliances that consume large amounts of energy. Opt for alternative methods like cooking on a portable stove or air-drying clothes.

Use natural light: Maximize the use of daylight by opening curtains and blinds during the day and relying on alternative lighting sources at night.

Passive Heating and Cooling Techniques

Passive heating and cooling techniques can help maintain comfortable indoor temperatures without relying on energy-intensive heating and cooling systems:

Insulation: Proper insulation in your home's walls, ceilings, and floors can help maintain stable indoor temperatures by reducing heat transfer.

Weatherstripping: Use weatherstripping to fill in gaps around your windows and doors. This stops drafts and unwanted outside air from sneaking in, helping you keep your home warmer or cooler.

Window treatments: Use curtains, blinds, or shades to regulate the amount of sunlight entering your home. During the winter, open window treatments to let in sunlight and close them at night to retain heat. In the summer, close window treatments during the day to block sunlight and open them at night to release heat.

Natural ventilation: Make the most of the breeze by opening your windows and doors when the weather's nice. This cross-ventilation not only freshens up your home but also cools it down naturally, reducing the need for air conditioning.

Thermal mass: Incorporate materials like brick or concrete in your home design. These materials are great at absorbing heat from the sun during the day and then releasing it slowly when it's cooler, keeping your house more temperature-stable without constant heating or cooling.

Key Takeaways

In this chapter, we explored various emergency power solutions. We discussed the pros and cons of alternative lighting sources, portable generators, solar power solutions, wind power solutions, and hydroelectric power systems. We also emphasized the importance of energy conservation and efficiency, highlighting strategies to reduce energy consumption.

Battery-powered LED lights, solar-powered options, oil lamps, candles, and glow sticks are versatile lighting options for power outages. Each has its advantages, such as energy efficiency, portability, or longevity, but also requires safety considerations and careful storage.

Portable generators come in gasoline, diesel, propane, and dual-fuel types, each offering different pros and cons regarding cost, efficiency, runtime, and portability. When choosing a generator, consider the total wattage of essential appliances to ensure sufficient power output and account for starting wattage in appliances. Regular maintenance and safety measures like proper ventilation and careful refueling are vital.

Solar power systems, primarily photovoltaic systems, are a sustainable way to generate electricity. Key considerations when choosing solar panels include type, efficiency, power output, size, durability, and cost. The efficiency of panels is crucial for converting sunlight into electricity effectively. Local regulations, incentives, and proper installation are also important factors to consider.

Solar generators and portable solar chargers provide portable, renewable energy and are especially useful for powering small devices.

Battery storage is vital for utilizing solar power effectively. Factors to consider include battery type, capacity, depth of discharge, cycle life, temperature tolerance, maintenance, and cost. Lead-acid and lithium-ion batteries are the most common types, each with distinct advantages and disadvantages.

Wind turbines are another renewable energy source, with options ranging from small-scale residential turbines to larger systems. Key considerations include assessing local wind resources, turbine size and power output, efficiency, budget, and compliance with local regulations. Regular maintenance and safety precautions are important for the longevity and effectiveness of wind turbines.

Micro-hydroelectric systems offer a continuous, low-impact power source for homes near water, requiring careful assessment of location, water flow, system efficiency, and regulatory compliance.

In the upcoming chapter, we'll explore the importance of safe water storage, effective sanitation practices, and how to ensure your family's access to clean water during a power outage. Stay tuned, as we continue to empower you with the tools and insights to keep you safe and secure in any situation.

Chapter Four

WATER STORAGE AND SANITATION

Thousands have lived without love, not one
without water.

W.H. Auden

Water is the essence of life, and its importance becomes even more evident during a power outage. This chapter will guide you through the critical aspects of water storage and sanitation. From storing an adequate supply of water to maintaining proper hygiene practices, we will provide you with the knowledge and practical tips to keep your family healthy and safe.

Water Storage

When a power outage strikes, access to clean water can become one of the most pressing concerns. This section will guide you through the process of determining your water storage needs, selecting appropriate containers, and maintaining water quality.

Determining water storage needs for your household

As a general rule of thumb, aim to store at least one gallon of water per person each day, and have enough for at least three days. However, individual needs may vary depending on factors like age, physical condition, and climate. To account for these factors, you might consider increasing your daily water storage target to two gallons per person. Remember to factor in the needs of pets, as they also require clean water for drinking.

Different types of water storage containers

When selecting water storage containers, choose options that are food-grade, BPA-free, and resistant to UV light to prevent the growth of algae. Some popular choices include:

Portable water containers: These are typically available in sizes from 1 to 7 gallons and can be easily transported during an evacuation.

Stackable water storage containers: Designed to save space, these containers are available in various sizes, usually holding between 3 and 5 gallons of water.

Water storage barrels: Larger in size, barrels can hold between 15 and 55 gallons of water and are suitable for long-term storage.

Ensure that containers are thoroughly cleaned and sanitized before filling them with water. Store containers in a cool, dark place, away from direct sunlight and potential contaminants.

Tips for maintaining water quality and safety

To maintain water quality during a power outage, follow these guidelines:

Keep water containers sealed with airtight lids to prevent contamination.

Regularly check the integrity of your water storage containers to ensure there are no leaks or damage.

Consider water preservers like chlorine dioxide to extend the shelf life of stored water. Follow the manufacturer's instructions for proper use.

Rotating water supplies and managing expiration dates

Stored water can go stale over time, so it's essential to rotate your water supply. Mark containers with the date they were filled and aim to replace stored water every six months to one year. If you have concerns about the quality of your stored water, consider testing it with a water quality test kit or purifying it before consumption.

Backup water sources that don't rely on electricity

In addition to storing water, it's wise to identify backup water sources in your area that do not depend on electricity, such as:

Rainwater collection systems: Install a rain barrel to collect water from your roof's downspouts.

Wells with manual pumps: If you have access to a well, consider installing a manual pump to extract water during power outages.

Nearby natural water sources: Identify nearby rivers, lakes, or streams that could be used as emergency water sources, keeping in mind that water from these sources will need to be treated before consumption.

By understanding your water storage needs and taking the necessary steps to maintain your water supply, you'll be better prepared to face a power outage with confidence. Remember, water is a vital resource during emergencies, and having an adequate supply on hand is crucial.

Water Purification

When a power outage occurs, the regular supply of clean water can be disrupted, making it essential to have a backup plan for water purification. This section will explore various methods of purifying water, as well as provide tips on how to choose the best method for your situation.

Boiling: A tried-and-true method for water purification

Boiling water is a reliable way to make it safe because it kills harmful pathogens like bacteria, viruses, and protozoa. When the power is out, you can still boil water using alternative heat sources, such as gas stoves, camping stoves, or grills. To ensure water safety, bring the water to a boil for at least one minute (or three minutes at higher elevations). Allow the water to cool naturally before consuming or storing it.

Chemical treatments: Disinfecting water with common household chemicals

Chemical treatments, such as chlorine bleach or iodine, can also be used to disinfect water. Follow these guidelines when using chemical treatments:

Chlorine bleach: Use unscented household bleach containing 5.25% to 6% sodium hypochlorite. For every gallon of water, mix in 1/8 teaspoon (or about 8 drops) of unscented bleach. Stir it well and let it sit for 30 minutes before you drink it.

Iodine: With 2% tincture of iodine, use 5 drops for each quart of clear water, or 10 drops if the water's cloudy. Mix it up and wait 30 minutes before drinking.

Water purification tablets: The two most common types of water purification tablets are iodine-based and chlorine-based tablets. Both types are effective in killing bacteria, viruses, and protozoa, but they have different taste profiles and shelf lives. Iodine-based tablets can leave a noticeable taste, while chlorine-based tablets tend to have a less pronounced taste. Some brands also offer chlorine dioxide tablets, which are effective against many microorganisms and leave minimal taste.Water purification tablets can be purchased at outdoor and camping stores, pharmacies, or online retailers. Look for reputable brands and ensure the tablets have a long shelf life, as they can last up to five years when stored properly.

Please note that chemical treatments may not be as effective against some parasites, like Cryptosporidium, and can affect the taste of the water.

Water filtration systems: Portable and gravity-fed options

Water filters are effective for purifying water during power outages. There are various portable and gravity-fed water filters available, designed to remove contaminants such as bacteria, viruses, and protozoa, as well as improve the taste and odor of the water. When selecting a water filter, consider factors like filtration speed, filter lifespan, and the specific contaminants the filter is designed to remove.

Portable water filters: These are lightweight, compact devices designed for individual use, often in the form of a straw or a water bottle with a built-in filter.

Pump filters: These filters require manual pumping to force water through the filter element. They are usually small and portable, making them suitable for backpacking or emergency situations.

Gravity-fed filters: These systems use gravity to pass water through a filter element, eliminating the need for manual pumping. They can filter larger quantities of water, making them ideal for families or groups.

Ceramic filters: These filters use a porous ceramic element to remove impurities from the water. They are often used in combination with other filtration methods, such as activated carbon, to improve taste and remove additional contaminants.

Activated carbon filters: They use activated carbon to clean the water, getting rid of contaminants and making it taste and smell better. They are often used in combination with other filtration methods, such as ceramic or hollow fiber filters.

When choosing portable or gravity-fed water filtration systems, consider the following tips:

Filter pore size: Look for a filter with a pore size of 0.2 microns or smaller, as it will effectively remove most bacteria, protozoa, and some viruses from the water.

Flow rate: Consider the flow rate of the system, which indicates how quickly the water passes through the filter. A higher flow rate is beneficial when filtering water for multiple people or when time is of the essence.

Filter lifespan: Check the filter's lifespan, usually indicated by the number of gallons or liters it can process before needing replacement. A longer lifespan means less frequent replacements and lower long-term costs.

Filter medium: Filters may use different types of media, such as activated carbon, ceramic, or hollow fiber. Each type has its pros and cons, so choose one that aligns with your needs and preferences. Activated carbon filters, for example, are great at removing unpleasant tastes and odors.

Ultraviolet (UV) purifiers and Solar water disinfection (SODIS)

UV purifiers use ultraviolet light to kill bacteria, viruses, and other microorganisms in the water. These devices are typically battery-powered, so ensure you have spare batteries during a power outage. Here are some tips on choosing a UV purifier:

Effectiveness: Look for a UV purifier that has been independently tested and certified to meet the standards set by organizations such as the NSF (National Sanitation Foundation) or the EPA (Environmental Protection Agency). These certifications ensure the purifier effectively eliminates waterborne pathogens.

Portability: Choose a purifier that is compact and lightweight. Some UV purifiers are designed to be used with water bottles, while others can be used with a variety of containers.

Battery life: Since UV purifiers rely on batteries for power, consider the battery life of the device. Look for purifiers with long-lasting, rechargeable batteries or ones that use common battery types like AA or AAA batteries, which are easy to find and replace. Additionally, consider the availability of alternative charging options, such as solar or USB.

Treatment time: The time required for a UV purifier to treat water can vary between devices. Opt for a purifier with a short treatment time (usually around 90 seconds or less), as this will allow for quicker access to clean water.

Solar water disinfection (SODIS) is a simple and low-cost method for purifying water that relies on sunlight to inactivate harmful pathogens. To perform SODIS, follow these steps:

- Fill clear plastic bottles (preferably PET bottles) with water.

- Place the bottles in direct sunlight for a minimum of 6 hours on a sunny day or up to 48 hours on a cloudy day.

- After the required exposure time, the water is considered safe to drink.

Keep in mind that SODIS is not effective in removing chemical contaminants or heavy metals from the water.

Water Purification Tips

1. Choosing the best water purification method for your situation during power outages

The most suitable water purification method for your situation will depend on factors such as the available resources, the quality of the water source, and the specific contaminants you need to remove. When selecting a method, consider the following:

- Availability: Ensure that you have access to the necessary equipment or supplies for the chosen method.

- Effectiveness: Choose a method that effectively targets the contaminants present in your water source.

- Ease of use: Opt for a method that is easy to use and understand, especially during a stressful situation like a power outage.

2. Combining water purification methods for increased effectiveness

In some cases, combining water purification methods can provide a more comprehensive approach to ensuring water safety. For example, using a water filter followed by boiling or chemical treatment can help remove both physical and biological contaminants.

3. Storing purified water safely during power outages

Once you have purified the water, it is crucial to store it properly to maintain its safety. Use clean, food-grade containers with tight-fitting lids to store the purified water. Store your water containers in a cool, shaded place, making sure they're not exposed to direct sunlight or contaminants. Change out the water every six months to keep it fresh.

In conclusion, having a reliable water purification strategy is essential during power outages. By understanding the various methods available and choosing the most appropriate method, you can ensure access to safe drinking water. Remember to consider factors like availability, effectiveness, and ease of use when selecting a water purification method, and always store your purified water safely to maintain its quality.

Personal Hygiene

In this section, we will discuss how to maintain proper sanitation and hygiene during a power outage, as well as practical tips to help you stay clean and healthy when water and electricity are scarce.

Maintaining personal hygiene with limited water resources and no power

Keeping yourself and your family clean during a power outage can be challenging, especially with limited water resources. Here are some tips to help you maintain personal hygiene during power outages:

Handwashing is a key way to stop diseases from spreading. If clean water is scarce, consider using alcohol-based hand sanitizers or disposable hand wipes as an alternative. Remember to wash your hands before handling food, after using the toilet, and after touching potentially contaminated surfaces.

Use wet wipes or baby wipes for quick cleaning of your body, particularly in areas prone to bacteria buildup, such as underarms and feet.

Use no-rinse body wash or shampoo to clean your hair and body without using much water.

Save water from washing fruits and vegetables or from cooking for personal hygiene purposes. Make sure to filter and boil the water before using it.

Wear clean clothes and change them regularly. If washing clothes is not an option, air them out in the sun to kill bacteria and reduce odors.

Toilet and waste disposal options

During a power outage, it's essential to have a plan for toilet and waste disposal, as sewage systems can become unreliable or stop functioning, especially if they rely on electricity to pump wastewater. While some homes may still have functioning toilets, there are alternative methods for waste disposal if the regular sewage system is down.

If your toilet is still functioning, you can use stored water to manually fill the tank and flush your waste. Simply pour the water into the tank until it reaches the fill line and then flush as usual. Keep in mind that you'll want to conserve water for other uses, so only flush when necessary.

However, if your sewage system is not functioning, you'll need alternative methods to dispose of human waste safely. Some options include:

• Portable camping toilets: These toilets are for outdoor use and can also work inside your home in an emergency. They are compact, self-contained, and usually come with disposable waste bags.

• Bucket toilets: A simple yet effective solution, bucket toilets can be made by lining a sturdy bucket with a heavy-duty garbage bag. Place a toilet seat or lid on top for added comfort. Be sure to seal the bags properly after each use and dispose of them in a designated waste area outside your home.

• Chemical toilets: These are similar to portable camping toilets but use chemicals to break down and deodorize waste. Chemical toilets can be purchased or improvised using a bucket, garbage bags, and a toilet seat. Follow the manufacturer's instructions for using and disposing of the chemicals.

- Digging a latrine: If you have outdoor space, you can dig a small latrine to bury human waste. Choose a location at least 200 feet away from any water source to prevent contamination. Dig a trench about 2-3 feet deep and cover the waste with soil after each use. Mark the area to prevent accidental exposure.

Preventing the spread of disease and maintaining health

To prevent the spread of disease and keep everyone healthy during power outages, follow these guidelines:

Keep your living space clean and tidy. Use disinfectant wipes or diluted bleach solution (1 cup of bleach per 5 gallons of water) to clean high-touch surfaces, such as countertops, doorknobs, and light switches.

Store food safely and discard any food that shows signs of spoilage.

Be cautious with water sources. If you're unsure about the quality of your water supply, treat it by boiling, filtering, or using water purification tablets.

Educate family members about proper sanitation and hygiene practices during power outages. Make sure everyone knows the importance of handwashing and maintaining personal cleanliness.

If someone in your family becomes ill, isolate them from other family members to prevent the spread of disease. Provide them with a designated area to rest, eat, and use the bathroom.

By following these tips, you can help ensure your family stays clean and healthy, even when water and electricity resources are limited.

Key Takeaways

Importance of water storage: Recognize the crucial role of water storage during power outages, and ensure that you have an adequate supply for drinking, cooking, and sanitation.

Water storage guidelines: Store at least one gallon of water per person per day for a minimum of three days and use food-grade water storage containers.

Rotating water storage: Regularly rotate your stored water supply to maintain freshness and prevent contamination.

Water purification methods: Familiarize yourself with various water purification techniques such as boiling, chemical treatment, and filtration, and select the most suitable method for your situation.

Importance of sanitation and hygiene: Understand the significance of maintaining proper sanitation and hygiene during power outages, especially when resources are limited.

Handwashing techniques and alternatives: Learn how to effectively wash your hands with limited water and electricity, and consider alternatives such as hand sanitizer and disposable wipes.

Maintaining personal hygiene: Adapt your personal hygiene routine to conserve water and work around the lack of power, including sponge baths and no-rinse cleansing products.

Toilet and waste disposal options: Explore different options for waste disposal, such as portable toilets, chemical toilets, and using stored water to flush conventional toilets if the sewage system is functional.

Preventing the spread of disease: Practice good sanitation and hygiene habits to minimize the risk of illness and maintain overall health during power outages.

By understanding and implementing these key takeaways, you can be better prepared to manage your water needs, ensuring your family's health and safety. In the next chapter, we will delve into food security, discussing storage and cooking techniques. Stay tuned for practical advice and useful tips to make sure you can weather any storm with a well-stocked pantry and an adaptable cooking strategy.

CHAPTER FIVE

FOOD STORAGE AND COOKING TECHNIQUES

One cannot think well, love well, sleep well,
if one has not dined well.

Virginia Woolf

In this chapter, we'll explore the ins and outs of storing food safely, cooking creatively without electricity, and ensuring that your family can still enjoy tasty and nutritious meals when the power grid fails.

Stocking Your Pantry

When it comes to food security during power outages, non-perishable and shelf-stable items are the MVPs. These foods have a long shelf life and don't require refrigeration, making them the perfect candidates for your emergency pantry. In this section, we'll provide you with a comprehensive list of non-perishable food items and offer tips on how to store them safely and efficiently.

Essential Non-Perishable Food Items

Building a well-stocked pantry begins with selecting the right non-perishable food items. Here are some essentials you should consider including in your emergency food supply:

Canned goods: Canned fruits, vegetables, beans, and soups are excellent options as they retain their nutritional value and are easy to prepare. Don't forget canned protein sources like tuna, chicken, or salmon.

Grains and pasta: Rice, pasta, quinoa, and couscous are versatile and can be used as a base for various dishes. Opt for whole grains whenever possible, as they offer higher nutritional value.

Dried beans and legumes: Lentils, chickpeas, and other dried beans are protein-rich, easy to store, and can be used in a variety of recipes.

Crackers and bread: Opt for whole grain crackers and shelf-stable bread options, such as tortillas, pita, or crispbreads, to add some crunch to your meals.

Snacks and treats: Granola bars, nuts, dried fruit, and trail mix are great for snacking on-the-go or as a pick-me-up during stressful times.

Nut butters and spreads: Peanut butter, almond butter, and other spreads are nutrient-dense, filling, and can be used in various ways.

Powdered milk and shelf-stable milk alternatives: These options are great for adding to coffee, tea, or cereal, and can also be used in cooking and baking.

Instant and ready-to-eat meals: Pre-packaged meals, such as freeze-dried camping food, instant noodles, or rice mixes, can be a lifesaver when you need a quick and easy meal.

Spices, seasonings, and condiments: Don't forget the flavor! Stock up on your favorite herbs, spices, salt, pepper, and condiments to keep your meals tasty and enjoyable.

Beverages: Powdered drink mixes, instant coffee, and tea bags are essential for staying hydrated and alert during a power outage.

Safe Storage Tips for Non-Perishable Foods

Once you've gathered your non-perishable food items, it's important to store them correctly to maximize their shelf life and ensure food safety. Here are some tips for proper food storage:

Keep foods in a cool, dry place: Excessive heat and moisture can shorten the shelf life of your non-perishable items, so store them away from direct sunlight and heat sources.

Use airtight containers: To prevent exposure to moisture, store items like grains, pasta, and snacks in airtight containers or resealable bags.

Keep your pantry organized: Group similar items together and use shelves or bins to keep your emergency food supply organized and easily accessible.

Label and date your items: Clearly label your non-perishable food items with their purchase date and expiration date to keep track of their shelf life.

Rotate your stock: Regularly use and replace the older items in your emergency stash with fresh purchases. This keeps everything up-to-date and safe to eat.

Regularly inspect your pantry: Frequently look over your stored food for any signs of spoilage, damage, or pest infestations. Get rid of anything that's contaminated or past its expiration date.

Special Dietary Needs and Preferences

When building emergency food supply, it's important to consider the dietary needs and preferences of your family members. Be sure to include:

Gluten-free and allergy-friendly options: Stock up on gluten-free grains, pasta, and snacks if anyone in your family has gluten sensitivity or allergies. Don't forget to include allergy-friendly alternatives, such as sunflower seed butter, if someone has a nut allergy.

Vegetarian and vegan options: Add a variety of plant-based proteins like beans, lentils, and tofu to cater to family members with vegetarian or vegan diets.

Baby and toddler foods: If you have young children, stock up on age-appropriate foods, such as baby cereals, purees, and toddler-friendly snacks.

Pet food: Don't forget about your furry family members! Keep an extra supply of pet food on hand.

Refrigerator and Freezer Management

Refrigerator and Freezer Tips

When a power outage occurs, one of your primary concerns may be how to keep your perishable foods cold and safe to eat. By following these tips, you can ensure that your refrigerator and freezer are prepared for power outages:

Keep your refrigerator and freezer full: A full refrigerator or freezer retains cold better than an empty one. If you don't have enough food to fill the space, consider adding containers of water to take up the extra room and help maintain the temperature.

Keep the refrigerator and freezer doors closed: Resist the temptation to open the doors frequently, as this allows cold air to escape. A refrigerator can typically maintain its temperature for up to four hours, while a full freezer can hold its temperature for up to 48 hours (24 hours if it's half full).

Use ice and coolers: If you know that a power outage will last longer than a few hours, consider transferring perishable foods to coolers with ice or ice packs. You can also use ice or ice packs in the refrigerator to help maintain its temperature.

Invest in appliance thermometers: Place thermometers in your refrigerator and freezer to monitor the temperature. If the temperature in the refrigerator rises above 40°F (4°C) for more than two hours or if the freezer temperature rises above 0°F (-18°C), it's time to take action to preserve your food.

Prioritize food consumption: If you suspect that a power outage may last for an extended period, prioritize consuming perishable foods first. This will help minimize food waste and ensure that you're eating the safest foods possible.

Food Safety Guidelines

During a power outage, it's essential to follow food safety guidelines to prevent foodborne illnesses. Here are some general tips to keep in mind:

When in doubt, throw it out: If you're unsure whether a perishable food item is still safe to eat, it's best to err on the side of caution and discard it. Consuming spoiled food can lead to illnesses, which can be especially dangerous during a power outage when medical resources may be limited.

Inspect your food carefully: Carefully inspect your perishable foods for signs of spoilage, such as off-odors or unusual textures. Discard any items that appear compromised.

Cook and consume thawed foods promptly: If perishable foods in your freezer have thawed but are still at or below 40°F (4°C), cook and consume them as soon as possible. Avoid refreezing thawed foods, as this can compromise their quality and safety.

Practice proper food handling: Always wash your hands and any surfaces that come into contact with food to minimize the risk of contamination.

By preparing your refrigerator and freezer for power outages and following proper food safety guidelines, you can help ensure that your perishable foods remain safe to eat during these challenging times. Taking the necessary precautions and being proactive in your food management strategies can make a significant difference in maintaining your family's health and well-being during a power outage.

Disposing of Spoiled Food after a Power Outage

Once the power has been restored, you may need to dispose of any spoiled food. Follow these guidelines for safe food disposal:

Wear gloves: To protect yourself from possible contamination, wear gloves while handling spoiled food.

Double-bag the food: Place spoiled food in a plastic bag, and then place that bag inside another one to prevent leaks and odors.

Dispose of the food properly: Follow your local waste disposal guidelines for disposing of spoiled food. Some communities may have specific requirements or designated drop-off locations for spoiled food disposal.

Clean and sanitize affected areas: After disposing of the spoiled food, clean and sanitize any areas that may have come into contact with it. This will help prevent the spread of bacteria and ensure a safe environment for your fresh food.

Alternative Cooking Methods

Propane or Gas Stoves

Propane or gas stoves are a popular choice for cooking during power outages, as they do not rely on electricity. These stoves can be used both indoors and outdoors, but proper ventilation is essential to prevent carbon monoxide poisoning. Make sure you have a reliable propane or gas supply on hand and familiarize yourself with the stove's operation before an emergency arises.

Portable Camping Stoves

Portable camping stoves are a versatile option for cooking. They typically use propane or butane fuel canisters and can be set up on a stable surface, both indoors and outdoors. Ensure you have adequate fuel and follow safety guidelines for using the stove, such as ensuring proper ventilation and avoiding flammable materials.

Charcoal or Wood Grills

Charcoal or wood grills can provide a means of cooking during a power outage. They are best used outdoors to avoid the risk of carbon monoxide poisoning. Ensure you have sufficient fuel (charcoal or wood) and a safe, well-ventilated area to set up the grill. Keep in mind that cooking times may vary from those of your regular stove or oven.

Dutch Ovens and Campfire Cooking

Using a Dutch oven or cooking over an open fire can be a fun and resourceful way to prepare meals. Dutch ovens are versatile cooking tools that can be used to make anything from stews and casseroles to baked goods. They are placed directly on coals or suspended over an open flame, making them perfect for outdoor cooking. When cooking over a campfire, ensure that you have a safe and contained fire area, and never leave the fire unattended.

Solar Ovens

Solar ovens use the energy of the sun to cook your food, making them an excellent option during power outages. They can reach temperatures of up to 300-400 degrees Fahrenheit (150-200 degrees Celsius), allowing you to cook a variety of dishes. When choosing a solar oven, consider factors such as size, weight, and ease of setup. Keep in mind that solar ovens require direct sunlight to function effectively, so they may not be suitable for use during cloudy or overcast weather.

Alcohol Stoves

Alcohol stoves are lightweight, portable, and easy to use. They typically run on denatured alcohol or other alcohol-based fuels, which are readily available and inexpensive. When using an alcohol stove, be aware that the flame may be nearly invisible, so exercise caution to avoid burns. As with other alternative cooking methods, ensure proper ventilation when using an alcohol stove indoors.

Biomass Stoves

Biomass stoves are an innovative and eco-friendly alternative cooking method that use organic materials such as twigs, leaves, wood pellets, or other small combustible materials as fuel. These stoves are designed to maximize the heat produced from burning biomass while minimizing the amount of smoke and harmful emissions. Biomass stoves come in various sizes and styles, ranging from portable models perfect for camping to larger, more permanent installations for home use. When using a biomass stove, ensure you have a readily available supply of fuel, maintain proper ventilation, and follow the manufacturer's safety guidelines to prevent accidents or injuries.

Canned Heat and Sterno

Canned heat, also known as Sterno or chafing fuel, is another alternative for cooking during power outages. These cans produce a steady flame that can be used to heat small pots and pans or to keep food warm. To use canned heat, simply light the wick or gel, place your cookware on a heat-resistant surface above the flame, and cook as needed. Remember to extinguish the flame when you're finished cooking and allow the can to cool before handling.

Safety Precautions for Alternative Cooking Methods

No matter which alternative cooking method you choose, always follow safety guidelines to prevent accidents, injuries, or carbon monoxide poisoning. These precautions include ensuring proper ventilation, using the cooking method in designated areas (preferably outdoors), and having a fire extinguisher or other fire safety equipment on hand. Additionally, never leave cooking appliances unattended, and keep children and pets away from the cooking area.

Check out these different cooking methods to keep your food supply steady and make sure your family gets warm meals. Learn the proper use and safety measures for each method to ensure you're prepared for any emergency.

Meal Planning and Preparation

Strategies for Creating Meal Plans

When preparing for a power outage, it's essential to have a meal plan in place that requires minimal resources and electricity. Here are some strategies for creating your meal plans:

Include easy-to-prepare foods: Look for foods that are simple to make and don't require much cooking, like instant oatmeal, canned soups, or pre-cooked rice.

Plan for meals that can be made with alternative cooking methods: As you create your meal plan, consider which dishes can be easily prepared using the alternative cooking methods discussed in the previous section.

Make a list of meals and snacks: Create a list of meals and snacks, so you have a clear idea of what you can prepare when the electricity is out.

Tips for Conserving Resources While Cooking

During a power outage, conserving resources is crucial. Here are some tips to help you minimize waste and make the most of your limited supplies:

Cook in bulk: If possible, cook large quantities of food at once to conserve fuel and make the most of your alternative cooking methods.

Utilize leftovers: Get creative with your leftovers to reduce waste and create new meals. For example, use leftover grilled vegetables in a salad or pasta dish.

Opt for one-pot meals: One-pot meals, like stews or casseroles, are an excellent way to save fuel and simplify the cooking process.

Keep lids on pots: Whenever you're cooking, keep the lids on pots to trap heat and reduce cooking time.

Ideas for No-Cook Meals and Snacks

In some cases, you may not have access to any cooking methods. Here are some tips for no-cook meals and snacks to help you stay nourished and satisfied:

Sandwiches and wraps: Use bread, tortillas, or pita pockets as a base and fill with canned meats, cheeses, or nut butter and jelly for a quick and easy meal.

Salads: Toss together canned beans, vegetables, and salad greens for a nutritious and filling salad. Add tuna, chicken, or salmon for extra protein.

Snack platters: Assemble a variety of non-perishable snacks, like crackers, cheese, nuts, and dried fruit, to create a satisfying and easy-to-prepare snack platter.

Overnight oats: Combine oats, shelf-stable milk or yogurt, and dried fruit or nuts in a container and let sit overnight for a ready-to-eat breakfast that doesn't require cooking.

Canned chili or stew: These ready-to-eat meals can be heated using alternative cooking methods or eaten cold if necessary.

Crackers and canned cheese spread: A simple and filling snack that doesn't require refrigeration.

Granola bars or energy bars: These shelf-stable snacks are a great source of energy and can be easily stored.

Canned fruits and vegetables: Canned produce is a great way to add fruits and vegetables into your diet, as they don't require refrigeration and have a long shelf life.

Instant rice or noodles: These quick-cooking options can be prepared using hot water from your alternative cooking methods.

Canned tuna or chicken salad: Mix canned tuna or chicken with mayonnaise (from a shelf-stable pouch) and serve on crackers or bread for a simple, protein-rich meal.

Trail mix: A combination of nuts, seeds, and dried fruit provides a high-energy snack that doesn't require refrigeration or cooking.

By planning ahead, you can ensure that your family have access to nutritious and satisfying meals during a power outage, even when your usual cooking methods aren't available.

Key Takeaways

In this chapter, we have explored various aspects of food security and cooking techniques during power outages. Here are the most important points to remember:

Stock up on non-perishable foods that have a long shelf life and require minimal preparation. This includes canned goods, dried fruits, nuts, granola bars, and other shelf-stable foods.

Properly store your perishable foods in the refrigerator and freezer to extend their freshness. Set the right temperature before a power outage, and avoid opening the doors frequently to maintain the cold air inside.

Make use of alternative cooking methods such as propane or gas stoves, charcoal or wood grills, Dutch ovens, solar ovens, portable camping stoves, alcohol stoves, and biomass stoves. Remember to follow safety precautions and ensure proper ventilation when using these methods.

Plan meals that require minimal resources and can be prepared using your alternative cooking methods. Conserve resources by cooking in bulk, reusing cooking water, and choosing no-cook meals and snacks when possible.

In the next chapter, we will discuss strategies for staying warm and maintaining a comfortable living environment, including alternative heating sources, insulation techniques, and tips for conserving heat in your home. Keep reading to learn how to stay safe and comfortable when the power goes out.

CHAPTER SIX

SHELTER AND WARMTH

In the depth of winter, I finally learned that
within me there lay an invincible summer.

Albert Camus

This chapter will guide you through various ways to create a
comfortable and safe environment when the power goes out.
From insulating your home and using alternative heating sources
to creating warmth without electricity, we'll cover some practical
strategies to help you face the cold with confidence.

Insulating Your Home

During a blackout, and you're left without heat, it's crucial to
have a well-insulated home to keep warm. Insulating your home
effectively can make the difference between a cozy hideaway and
a chilly nightmare. Let's look at some insulation techniques that
can help you stay warm and maybe even save you some money in
the long run.

Window insulation techniques

Windows can be notorious culprits for heat loss, but don't worry, there are ways to combat those sneaky drafts. Here are some techniques that can help you insulate your windows:

Weatherstripping: Apply adhesive-backed foam tape around the window frames to seal any gaps.

Window film: This magical stuff can be applied to your windows to reduce heat transfer. It's like plastic wrap for your windows but without the frustration of it sticking to everything else.

Insulated curtains or thermal blinds: These can trap heat and give your room a cozy atmosphere. They're like snuggly blankets for your windows.

Draft snakes: Channel your inner DIY spirit and create draft snakes with fabric and filling. These little guys can be placed at the bottom of your windows to block drafts.

Door insulation and draft stoppers

Doors can let in drafts that send shivers down your spine. Here's how to insulate your doors and keep the cold at bay:

Weatherstripping: Similar to windows, apply adhesive-backed foam tape around the door frame to seal gaps. It's like giving your door a warm hug.

Door sweeps: Attach a sweep to the bottom of the door to prevent drafts. Say goodbye to those cold breezes sneaking in under the door.

Draft stoppers: Create or purchase draft stoppers, like those for windows, to block drafts at the bottom of the door.

Using curtains, blankets, and rugs to conserve heat

Here are some new ways to use everyday items for temporary insulation:

Hang heavy curtains or blankets over windows and doors to trap heat.

Close curtains and blinds at night to retain warmth, and open them during the day to let in sunlight. It's like giving your home a suntan while it's cold outside.

Use area rugs or carpets to insulate cold floors. Your feet will thank you.

Hang blankets or quilts on walls to add an extra layer of insulation.

Long-term solutions for energy efficiency

While temporary insulation techniques can help during a power outage, it's essential to consider long-term solutions for energy efficiency:

Upgrading insulation materials: Consider investing in higher-quality insulation materials like spray foam, blown-in cellulose, or rigid foam boards to improve your home's ability to keep heat in. Additionally, you may want to use advanced insulation methods like insulating concrete forms (ICFs) or structural insulated panels (SIPs) when constructing or renovating your home for enhanced energy efficiency.

Upgrade to energy-efficient windows and doors: They help keep the heat inside your home. Choose ones with double or triple glazing, low-emissivity (low-E) coatings, and argon or krypton gas fills to really lock in the warmth. Similarly, opt for insulated doors with high R-values (thermal resistance) to minimize heat loss.

Fill any gaps or cracks on the outside of your house: Check around for gaps, cracks, or openings that might let cold air sneak in. Use caulking and weatherstripping to seal these gaps, especially around windows, doors, and other openings like vents or electrical outlets. This easy step can significantly reduce drafts and improve your home's overall insulation.

Adding a programmable thermostat to regulate your home's temperature efficiently: A programmable thermostat can help you maintain a comfortable temperature in your home while conserving energy. Adjust your thermostat to lower settings when you're out or sleeping, and make it warmer when you're home and awake.

Considering a home energy management system to optimize energy consumption: A home energy management system (HEMS) is a smart technology that monitors your home's energy usage and provides insights and recommendations to improve energy efficiency. By using a HEMS, you can identify areas of energy waste, optimize your home's energy consumption, and better prepare for potential power outages. Some HEMS even allow you to control your home's heating and cooling remotely, providing added convenience and control over your home's temperature.

By implementing these long-term solutions, you can not only keep your home warm and comfortable but also save on energy costs and reduce carbon footprint. Remember, an energy-efficient home is a happy home, and being well-prepared for a power outage can make all the difference in your comfort and safety.

Alternative Heating Sources

Wood-burning stoves and fireplaces

Wood-burning stoves and fireplaces can be a reliable and cozy alternative heating source. When using these methods, be sure to have a well-stocked supply of dry, seasoned wood on hand. If you have a fireplace, make sure it is properly maintained, with a clean chimney and flue to prevent potential fire hazards and carbon monoxide poisoning. When using a wood-burning stove, ensure it meets EPA emission standards and is professionally installed, as proper ventilation is crucial.

Wood-burning stoves and fireplaces can provide a significant amount of heat and ambiance during a power outage. Here are some additional details to consider when using these heating sources:

Types of wood-burning stoves: There are two main types of wood-burning stoves: catalytic and non-catalytic. Catalytic stoves use a ceramic honeycomb to lower the combustion temperature, reducing emissions and increasing efficiency. Non-catalytic stoves create a hot fire, relying on insulation and a large baffle to extend the burn. Both types have their pros and cons, so research and choose the best option for your needs.

Fireplace inserts: If you have a masonry fireplace, consider installing a fireplace insert, which can greatly improve heat output and efficiency. These inserts are designed to fit inside your fireplace and provide a sealed combustion chamber, allowing more heat to radiate into your living space.

Wood selection: Choose hardwoods like oak, hickory, or maple, as they provide more heat and burn longer compared to soft-woods like pine or spruce. Store wood in a dry, covered area to prevent moisture from reducing its burning efficiency.

Fireplace maintenance: Regularly remove ashes and clean the firebox to maintain efficient burning. Inspect the damper to ensure it opens and closes properly, and consider adding a chimney cap to prevent debris or critters from entering the chimney.

Propane and kerosene heaters

Propane and kerosene heaters come with their own set of safety considerations. Only use propane heaters designed for indoor use, and never use a propane or kerosene heater in an enclosed space with poor ventilation, as they can produce deadly carbon monoxide. Always follow the manufacturer's guidelines for usage and fuel storage, and keep a fire extinguisher nearby in case of emergencies.

Propane and kerosene heaters offer powerful and portable heating options. Here are some additional details to consider when using these heaters:

Types of propane heaters: They come in various styles, including forced air, radiant, and convection. Forced air heaters blow hot air into the space, while radiant heaters emit infrared heat, warming objects and people directly. Convection heaters spread warm throughout the room. Consider your needs and the size of the space to determine the best option for you.

Kerosene heater efficiency: Kerosene heaters are generally more efficient than propane heaters, providing more heat per unit of fuel. However, kerosene can be more difficult to find and store, so consider the availability of fuel when choosing a heater.

Fuel storage: Store propane and kerosene in approved containers in a well-ventilated place, away from heat sources and living spaces. Check local regulations for fuel storage limits and requirements.

Heater maintenance: Regularly clean and inspect your propane or kerosene heater according to the manufacturer's instructions. Replace damaged parts as needed to maintain safe and efficient operation.

Portable electric heaters (with a backup power source)

Portable electric heaters can be an excellent option for heating individual rooms during a power outage, provided you have a backup power source, such as a generator or battery backup system. These heaters come in various types, including convection, infrared, and oil-filled radiators. Choose a heater with built-in safety features like a tip-over switch and overheat protection, and keep flammable materials at a safe distance.

Additional alternative heating sources

Bioethanol fireplaces: Bioethanol fireplaces burn a clean, eco-friendly fuel made from plant-derived ethanol. They produce no smoke or ash, and many models are portable and easy to set up. However, bioethanol fireplaces may not provide as much heat as other alternative heating sources.

Gel fuel fireplaces: Similar to bioethanol fireplaces, gel fuel fireplaces use a gel-based fuel that burns cleanly and produces no smoke or ash. They are also portable and easy to set up. While they provide some heat, it may not be sufficient for larger spaces or extended periods of cold weather.

Battery-powered heating pads or blankets: While not a primary heating source, battery-powered heating pads or blankets can provide personal warmth during a power outage. They can be especially helpful for keeping young children, elderly family members, or individuals with health conditions warm and comfortable.

DIY improvised heaters: In an emergency, you can create a makeshift heater using everyday items like terracotta pots, bricks, and candles. These heaters work by trapping and radiating the heat generated by the candles. Keep in mind that these improvised heaters are not as efficient or safe as commercially-available alternatives, so use them only in well-ventilated spaces and with extreme caution.

Safety precautions when using alternative heating sources

Regardless of which alternative heating source you choose, it's crucial to prioritize safety. Here are some general safety precautions to keep in mind:

Ventilation: Ensure proper ventilation to avoid carbon monoxide poisoning. This is especially important when using wood-burning stoves, fireplaces, and propane or kerosene heaters. Regularly check and maintain your home's carbon monoxide detectors.

Fire safety: Keep a fire extinguisher nearby and make sure all household members know how to use it. Regularly inspect and clean chimneys, flues, and wood-burning stoves. Store fuel for heaters in approved containers and in a well-ventilated area away from heat sources.

Safe operation: Follow the manufacturer's guidelines for using and maintaining your chosen heating source. Do not leave heaters unattended or operate them while you're asleep. Keep children and pets at a safe distance from heat sources.

Proper installation: If you choose to install a more permanent alternative heating source, such as a wood-burning stove, have it professionally installed to ensure proper ventilation and safety measures.

Backup power: If you're using electric heaters, make sure you have a reliable backup power source, like a generator or battery backup system. Keep in mind that generators should be placed outdoors, away from windows and doors, to prevent carbon monoxide buildup.

Creating Warmth without Electricity

Use heat packs

Heat packs, also known as hand warmers, foot warmers, or body warmers, can provide additional warmth. These portable heat sources are typically made of a combination of iron powder, water, activated carbon, vermiculite, and salt, which generates heat through an exothermic reaction when exposed to air.

To activate a heat pack, follow the instructions on the packaging, which usually involve shaking or squeezing the pack. Once activated, the heat pack will begin to warm up and can generate heat for several hours, depending on the specific product. Place the heat packs inside gloves, pockets, socks, or under blankets to help keep your extremities warm.

Some heat packs are reusable and can be reactivated by boiling them in water or microwaving them (when the power is back on), while others are disposable and should be discarded after use. Be sure to read the instructions carefully and follow any safety precautions provided by the manufacturer.

Keep a supply of heat packs in your emergency preparedness kit, and make sure everyone in the household knows where to find them and how to use them.

Layering clothing for optimal warmth

Staying warm without electricity means dressing right. Wearing layers is key to keeping your body heat in and staying cozy. Begin with a base layer that wicks away sweat, like polyester or merino wool, to stay dry. Steer clear of cotton because it holds moisture and might leave you feeling colder.

Next, put on a warm layer to hold in the heat, like a fleece jacket or a wool sweater. Finally, wear an outer layer to protect you from wind and moisture, such as a waterproof and windproof jacket or coat. Don't forget to protect your hands, feet, and head, as these areas lose heat more rapidly than the rest of your body. Wear warm socks, insulated gloves or mittens, and a hat to cover your ears.

Remember that it's better to wear multiple light layers rather than a single heavy one. This allows you to adjust your clothing based on your activity level and the indoor temperature.

Using blankets, sleeping bags, and emergency blankets

Blankets and sleeping bags can provide additional warmth. Pile on the blankets on your bed, couch, or wherever you're resting to create a cozy cocoon of warmth. When choosing blankets, opt for materials that offer good insulation, such as wool, fleece, or down. Layer them in a way that traps heat effectively, with the heaviest blankets on top and lighter ones underneath.

Sleeping bags are designed for outdoor camping and can provide exceptional warmth in cold conditions. If you have a sleeping bag rated for low temperatures, consider using it during a power outage to stay warm. Mummy-style sleeping bags, which are tapered at the feet and have a hood to cover the head, are particularly effective at retaining body heat.

Emergency blankets, also called space blankets or Mylar blankets, are lightweight, compact, and can reflect up to 90% of your body heat back to you. They are made of a thin, reflective material that helps to trap heat and can be used in addition to your regular blankets or sleeping bags. Drape an emergency blanket over your bed, wrap it around yourself, or even tape it to your windows to help insulate your home.

Close off unused rooms and create a "warm room":

Closing off unused rooms is a simple but effective way to conserve heat in your home during a power outage. By shutting doors to rooms you aren't using, you can prevent cold air from circulating throughout the house and concentrate your efforts on maintaining warmth in a smaller area.

To create a "warm room," designate a single room in your home as the primary gathering space. Ideally, choose a room with minimal windows and doors, as this will help reduce heat loss. Insulate this room as much as possible, using the techniques mentioned earlier, such as sealing gaps around windows and doors, covering windows with clear plastic film or bubble wrap, and using draft stoppers.

Place blankets, sleeping bags, and pillows on the floor or furniture to create a comfortable and cozy space for everyone to gather. You can also hang blankets or heavy curtains over the doorways to help insulate the room further. Ensure that everyone knows that this is the designated "warm room" and that they should stay in this area as much as possible during the power outage.

Protecting Your Home and Pipes from Freezing

Preparing your home's exterior for cold weather

To protect your home from freezing, you should prepare its exterior before cold weather strikes. Here are some steps to take:

Keep gutters and downspouts clean to allow water to flow freely and avoid the build-up of ice dams, which can cause water to leak into your home.

Check your roof for any signs of damage like missing shingles and repair them. Also, look for any water damage, mold, or rot in your attic or ceilings.

Fill any gaps or cracks in your home's exterior, including around windows and doors, with caulk or weatherstripping to keep drafts out and maintain warmth inside. Pay special attention to areas around electrical outlets, vents, and pipes.

Install storm windows or window film to provide an extra layer of insulation. These can also help reduce heat loss through your windows.

Trim tree branches that may pose a hazard to your home during heavy snow or ice storms. Falling branches can cause damage to your roof or siding and lead to water infiltration.

Disconnect and drain hoses, and turn off the water to outdoor faucets to prevent freezing. Use insulated faucet covers for added protection.

Insulating and protecting pipes from freezing

To prevent pipes from freezing, follow these steps:

Insulate exposed pipes in unheated places, such as basements, crawl spaces, garages, and attics, using pipe insulation or foam sleeves. Be sure to cover all joints and bends.

Seal gaps and cracks around pipes that run through exterior walls to prevent drafts and cold air from entering. Use expanding foam insulation or caulk for a tight seal.

Leave the cabinet doors open under your sinks to let warm air move around the pipes. Place a small portable heater nearby for added warmth if needed.

Safe use of heat tape and pipe insulation

Heat tape, also known as heat cable or pipe heating cable, can be an effective way to prevent pipes from freezing. However, it's important to use heat tape safely and correctly:

Choose heat tape that is designed for your type of pipes (copper, PVC, etc.) and follow the manufacturer's instructions for installation. Some heat tapes are self-regulating, while others require a separate thermostat.

Do not use heat tape on damaged or leaking pipes, as this can pose a fire hazard. Repair or replace damaged pipes before applying heat tape.

Use a thermostat-controlled heat tape to regulate the temperature and prevent overheating. Make sure the thermostat is placed on the coldest section of the pipe for accurate temperature readings.

Inspect the heat tape regularly for any signs of wear or damage, and replace it when needed. Look for frayed wires, cracked insulation, or damaged heating elements.

Avoid overlapping the heat tape or wrapping it too tightly, as this can cause overheating and damage the tape. Ensure the tape is evenly spaced and properly secured to the pipe.

Key Takeaways

In this chapter, we have explored various strategies to maintain shelter and warmth during a power outage. The key takeaways include:

Insulating your home: Implement window insulation techniques, door insulation and draft stoppers, insulating walls and ceilings, and using curtains, blankets, and rugs to conserve heat. Consider long-term insulation solutions for energy efficiency.

Alternative heating sources: Utilize wood-burning stoves and fireplaces, propane and kerosene heaters, or portable electric heaters with a backup power source. Always follow safety precautions when using these alternative heating sources.

Creating warmth without electricity: Layer clothing for optimal warmth, use blankets, sleeping bags, and emergency blankets, close off unused rooms, and employ heat packs to stay warm.

Protecting your home and pipes from freezing: Prepare your

home's exterior for cold weather, insulate and protect pipes from freezing, use heat tape and pipe insulation safely, and know what to do if your pipes freeze.

By taking these measures, you can ensure your family's comfort and safety in cold weather. In the next chapter, we will discuss the importance of being prepared for medical emergencies during a crisis, including having a well-stocked first aid kit, knowing basic first aid skills, and understanding how to manage chronic medical conditions.

Chapter Seven

MEDICAL PREPAREDNESS

Health is the greatest gift, contentment
the greatest wealth, faithfulness the best
relationship.

Buddha

Accidents can happen anytime during a power outage, and being prepared with essential first aid skills and supplies can make a huge difference in a crisis. In this chapter, we will discuss how to maintain your family's well-being during power outages by learning vital first aid skills, building a comprehensive first aid kit, managing chronic medical conditions, and taking care of your mental health. By equipping yourself with this knowledge and preparing in advance, you can face any crisis with confidence.

Essential First Aid Skills

Power outages often increase accident and injury risks due to the lack of lighting, disrupted routines, and the use of alternative heat and light sources. In such situations, having essential first aid skills can make a difference. Knowing what to do in the crucial moments following an injury can save lives and prevent complications.

Basic first aid principles

Understanding basic first aid principles is crucial in handling emergencies effectively. Here's how you can apply these principles:

Assess the Situation: Check the area around you and the injured person for safety before you step in. Identify hazards like fire, traffic, or electricity before approaching.

Call for Help: If the situation is beyond your capability or the person needs professional medical attention, call emergency services immediately.

Provide Care - Remember the ABCs:

• Airway: Ensure the person's airway is clear. If they are unconscious, gently tilt their head back and lift their chin to open the airway. Look for obstructions and be prepared to clear their mouth if necessary.

• Breathing: Check if the person is breathing. Look for chest movements, listen for breath sounds, and feel for air on your cheek. If they are not breathing normally, begin CPR if trained, or provide rescue breaths if applicable.

• Circulation: Address any bleeding or circulation issues. If you find severe bleeding, place a clean cloth or bandage firmly over the wound and apply direct pressure on it. Look for signs of shock like pale, cold skin and treat accordingly by laying the person down and elevating their legs, if there are no injuries preventing this.

Remember, providing first aid is about doing the best you can under the circumstances. Stay calm, and don't hesitate to ask others for help. Regularly refreshing your knowledge and skills in a certified first aid course is highly recommended to be prepared for emergencies.

CPR and AED

With disrupted communication and delayed emergency services during a power outage, knowing cardiopulmonary resuscitation (CPR) can be a life-saving skill. CPR is a technique used when someone's heart stops beating or they are not breathing effectively. It involves chest compressions and rescue breaths to circulate blood to the brain and vital organs. An automated external defibrillator (AED) is a device that can help restart the heart by delivering an electrical shock. Familiarize yourself with CPR and AED usage by taking a certified course.

If an AED is available, turn it on and follow the voice prompts. It will guide you through the process of attaching the pads, analyzing the heart rhythm, and delivering a shock if necessary.

To learn more about CPR and AED, the American Heart Association (AHA) and the American Red Cross offer certified courses that teach lifesaving skills, including CPR, AED, and first aid. These courses are available online and in-person, and some are specifically designed for laypersons, while others are tailored for healthcare professionals. You can find local classes or online courses by visiting the websites of the AHA (www.heart.org) and the American Red Cross (www.redcross.org). Certification is generally valid for two years, after which you will need to take a refresher course to maintain your skills and knowledge.

Choking

During a power outage, people may resort to eating non-perishable foods that could increase the risk of choking. The Heimlich maneuver is often used to clear a blocked airway. Learn how to perform the Heimlich maneuver on adults, children, and infants, and be prepared to act quickly in a choking situation.

To learn how to perform the maneuver on adults, children, and infants, it is advisable to seek formal training from certified professionals or organizations. Many local health organizations, community centers, and hospitals offer first aid and CPR courses that include training in the Heimlich maneuver.

While in-person training is recommended, if you need to learn it by yourself, you can utilize reputable online resources. Many health organizations, including the American Red Cross and the American Heart Association, offer detailed guides, instructional videos, and even interactive online courses that cover the Heimlich maneuver. These resources typically provide step-by-step instructions for performing the maneuvers.

Wound care

Cuts, scrapes, and puncture wounds can occur during a power outage, especially when navigating in the dark or handling tools. Learn how to properly clean and dress a wound, when to use adhesive strips or sutures, and when to seek professional medical attention.

For minor cuts and scrapes: Clean the wound with water to remove any debris gently. If you're not allergic, apply an antibiotic ointment on it. Next, cover it up with a sterile adhesive bandage or gauze, securing it with some medical tape. Make sure to change the dressing each day or when it gets wet or dirty. Keep an eye out for any infection signs, like increased redness, swelling, or any pus.

For deeper wounds: Press down on the wound using a clean cloth or gauze to control bleeding. Try to keep the injured area raised above heart if you can. And if the wound's deep, large, or won't stop bleeding after a steady 10 minutes of pressure, it's time to get professional medical help.

Burns

The risk of burns increases during a power outage due to the use of candles, cooking on open flames, or contact with hot surfaces. Know how to recognize and treat different degrees of burns, including first, second, and third-degree burns. Familiarize yourself with proper burn care, such as cooling the burn, applying burn ointment, and dressing the wound.

For minor (first-degree) burns:

- Cool the burn under cold running water for at least 10 minutes or until the pain subsides.

- Use aloe vera gel or an over-the-counter burn ointment to soothe the skin.

- Cover the burn area with a sterile, non-stick bandage or gauze.

- Take over-the-counter pain relievers if necessary.

For more severe (second and third-degree) burns, seek immediate medical attention. Do not attempt to self-treat

Fractures and sprains

Fractures and sprains can occur as people may trip or fall in the dark or engage in physical activities. Know how to spot fractures or sprains, and learn to stabilize the injury with a splint or sling. Know when to seek professional medical help for such injuries.

- Keep the injured area still and avoid moving the injured limb.

- If a bone is protruding, do not attempt to push it back into place.

- Apply ice wrapped in a cloth to the injured area to help reduce swelling. Do not apply ice directly to the skin.

- If you suspect a fracture, seek medical help right away. If you suspect a sprain and symptoms do not improve within 24-48 hours, consult a healthcare professional.

Other first aid skills

In addition to the above skills, consider learning other essential first aid techniques such as recognizing and treating signs of heatstroke, hypothermia, dehydration, and shock. It's also essential to know when to seek medical help and when to call emergency services. The more first aid knowledge you have, the better equipped you will be to handle medical emergencies.

By mastering these essential skills, you can be prepared to provide care and support. Remember that proper training is crucial, and consider taking a certified first aid course to ensure you have the skills and knowledge necessary to handle a variety of medical situations.

Building a Comprehensive First Aid Kit.

Having a well-stocked and properly maintained first aid kit can make all the difference in addressing minor injuries or even saving a life. Here's how to build a first aid kit tailored to your family's needs and ensure its effectiveness during an emergency.

Essential items for a first aid kit

A basic first aid kit should contain the following items:

- Adhesive bandages in various sizes
- Sterile gauze pads and rolls
- Adhesive tape
- Tweezers and scissors
- Safety pins
- Disposable gloves
- Digital thermometer
- Instant cold packs
- Antiseptic wipes and solution
- Hydrogen peroxide
- Antibiotic ointment
- Burn cream or gel
- Sterile saline solution for eye wash
- Elastic (ACE) bandages for sprains and strains
- Pain relievers (aspirin, ibuprofen, or acetaminophen)
- Antihistamine for allergic reactions

- Hydrocortisone cream for rashes and insect bites

- A first aid manual or guide

Tailoring your first aid kit to your family's needs

To customize your first aid kit for your family, consider the following factors:

Medical conditions: Include specific medications or supplies for family members with chronic conditions like diabetes, asthma, or allergies.

Age of family members: Include age-appropriate items, such as pediatric medications for children and smaller bandages for their smaller limbs.

Pets: Don't forget to include supplies for your pets, such as pet-specific bandages and medication.

Storing and maintaining your first aid kit

Proper storage and maintenance of your first aid kit are crucial for its effectiveness during a power outage.

- Store the kit in a cool, dry place, away from direct sunlight or extreme temperatures.

- Keep the kit in a sturdy, waterproof container that is easy to carry and access.

- Regularly check the contents of the kit for expired medications, damaged items, or depleted supplies.

- Replace any used or expired items promptly.

Emergency medications to include

During a power outage, access to prescription medications may be limited, so it's essential to have a supply of emergency medications in your first aid kit. Consult with your healthcare provider about the specific medications that are appropriate for your family. Some common emergency medications to consider include:

- Prescription medications for chronic conditions (e.g., insulin, asthma inhalers, or blood pressure medications)

- Over-the-counter medications for pain relief, fever, and inflammation

- Anti-diarrheal medications and oral rehydration salts

- Antacids and acid reducers for heartburn and indigestion

- Decongestants and cough suppressants for cold and flu symptoms

By building a comprehensive first aid kit tailored to your family's needs and maintaining it regularly, you'll be well-prepared to handle minor injuries or medical emergencies.

Managing Chronic Medical Conditions

During a blackout, managing chronic medical conditions can become more challenging. It's important to have a plan for ongoing care, keeping your medications stocked, and staying in touch with your doctors. Here are some strategies to help you manage chronic medical conditions:

Maintaining medication supply and storage

Maintain at least a two-week supply of essential prescription medications, and store them in a cool, dry place in airtight containers. If possible, keep an updated list of medications, dosages, and any known allergies.

Regularly rotate your medication stock to avoid using expired medications during an emergency. Check expiration dates and replace any expired ones promptly.

For medications that require refrigeration, such as insulin, use insulated containers or coolers with ice packs to maintain the proper temperature during a power outage. Regularly check the temperature inside the cooler and replace ice packs as needed.

Use battery-operated pill organizers to help you stay on schedule with medication doses. Make sure you have spare batteries for these devices.

Monitoring devices and backup power sources

For battery-operated monitoring devices, such as blood glucose meters or blood pressure monitors, keep a supply of spare batteries on hand. Check the battery life of your devices and replace them as needed.

For medical equipment that requires electricity, such as oxygen concentrators or CPAP machines, have a backup power like a generator or battery backup system. Make sure you have enough fuel for the generator and that it is properly maintained.

If possible, have a manual alternative for essential medical equipment. For example, keep a manual blood pressure cuff for use when an electronic one is not operational.

Communicating with healthcare providers during an outage

Discuss a communication plan with your healthcare providers. This plan should include alternative methods of communication, such as texting, using landlines, or visiting the provider's office in person if necessary.

Keep a list of emergency contacts, including your healthcare providers, pharmacists, and any specialists involved in your care. Have both their office and emergency contact numbers readily available.

If you have a medical alert system, ensure that it has a battery backup and that the batteries are in good working order. Test the system often to ensure it is functioning properly.

By taking these steps, you can effectively manage chronic medical conditions. This proactive approach will help maintain your health and well-being, even in challenging circumstances.

Mental Health and Coping Strategies

Power outages can bring about a mix of physical and mental challenges. It's crucial to address not only the inconveniences but also the psychological impact on everyone involved.

Ways to handle stress and anxiety

Deep breathing exercise: Slow, deep breaths can help calm the nervous system and reduce stress. Encourage everyone in the family to practice deep breathing exercises together.

Muscle relaxation: Tense and relax various muscle groups in the body to release tension. This can be done individually or as a group activity.

Mindfulness and meditation: Engage in mindfulness practices, focusing on the present and observing thoughts and feelings without judgment. Guided meditation can help introduce these practices.

Create a calming environment: Use battery-powered candles or low lighting to create a soothing atmosphere. Encourage everyone to find a comfortable spot and engage in activities, such as reading or listening to calming music.

Key Takeaways

In this chapter, we explored the importance of medical preparedness. The key takeaways from this chapter include:

Essential first aid skills: Learn and practice basic first aid principles, CPR and AED, choking response, wound care, burn treatment, and fracture and sprain management to be prepared for emergencies during a power outage.

Building a comprehensive first aid kit: Tailor your first aid kit to your family's needs, store and maintain it properly, and include essential items and emergency medications.

Managing chronic medical conditions: Ensure that you have a sufficient supply of medications, access to monitoring devices, and backup power sources. Maintain communication with healthcare providers during an outage.

Mental health and coping strategies: Recognize signs of stress and anxiety in yourself and others, and employ techniques to manage these emotions.

In the next chapter, we will dive into the critical aspect of maintaining communication during a grid-down situation. We will explore various communication methods, devices, and systems, as well as discuss strategies for staying connected with loved ones and emergency services.

Chapter Eight

COMMUNICATION AND CONNECTIVITY

Alone we can do so little; together we can do
so much.

Helen Keller

Communication is essential not only for getting help and sharing information, but also for ensuring the safety of everyone affected. During an extended power outage, traditional communication methods, such as cell phones and internet services, may be unreliable or unavailable. As a result, it is crucial to explore alternative communication methods.

This chapter will guide you through various communication options and technologies that can help you stay connected. We will discuss both conventional and unconventional methods, including two-way radios, satellite phones, hand-crank radios, and other low-tech solutions. Moreover, we will provide tips on selecting the right communication devices and systems, as well as guidelines on using them safely and effectively.

Landline Phones

Pros and Cons of Landline Phones

Landline phones, particularly corded ones, can be a reliable form of communication. One major advantage of traditional landline phones is that they do not rely on the electrical grid for power, which means they can continue to work during a power outage. Additionally, landline phones offer a more stable connection compared to cell phones, which can suffer from signal loss or network congestion during emergencies. Furthermore, landline phones provide direct access to emergency services (911), making it easier to call for help when needed.

However, there are also some drawbacks to using landline phones. For one, unlike cell phones, landline phones are restricted to a fixed location, which can be a disadvantage if you need to leave your home. Secondly, landline phones rely on physical lines that can be damaged during natural disasters, making them susceptible to service disruptions.

Preparing Your Landline Phone for Emergencies

To ensure that your landline phone is ready for emergencies, make sure to have at least one corded landline phone in your home. Also, keep a handy list of important phone numbers (family, friends, local authorities, and utility companies) near your phone so that you have quick access to these contacts. Lastly, regularly check that your landline phone is functioning correctly to ensure it will work during an emergency.

Cell Phones and Mobile Networks

Cell phones and mobile networks can still be useful when the grid goes down. However, there are limitations to consider. During a widespread power outage, cell towers may also be affected, leading to weak or no signal in certain areas. Additionally, heavy network congestion due to increased call volume may result in dropped calls or slow data speeds.

To overcome some of these limitations, it's essential to have strategies in place for conserving your phone's battery life. Start by turning off non-essential features like Wi-Fi, Bluetooth, and GPS when not in use. Adjusting screen brightness to the lowest comfortable setting and enabling battery-saving modes can also help prolong battery life. Limit the use of power-hungry apps and refrain from streaming videos or engaging in other high-data activities.

When using mobile networks for communication, keep in mind that text messages are more likely to get through during times of network congestion compared to voice calls. Furthermore, texts use less battery power than voice calls, making them an efficient option for communication. If voice communication is necessary, consider using data-based apps like WhatsApp, Signal, or Skype, as they may still function even if the cellular network is congested.

It's crucial to have a backup power source for your cell phone. Portable chargers and battery packs can provide extra power when needed. Look for high-capacity battery packs that offer multiple full charges for your device. Solar-powered chargers can also be a valuable option, as they can recharge devices using sunlight.

In summary, while cell phones and mobile networks may have limitations, they can still serve as a valuable communication tool. By conserving battery life, using text messages for communication, and having backup power sources, you can stay connected during a power outage.

Two-Way Radios

Two-way radios are crucial for staying in touch, particularly when cell phones and landlines are not operational. There are several types of two-way radios, each with their own advantages and limitations. In this section, we will explore walkie-talkies, CB radios, FRS/GMRS radios, and HAM radios, along with range, power, frequency considerations, licensing requirements, and tips for effective communication.

Types of two-way radios

Walkie-talkies: These are portable, handheld devices that are easy to use and widely available. They are suitable for short-range communication, usually up to a few miles, depending on terrain and obstructions. Walkie-talkies typically operate on FRS (Family Radio Service) frequencies, which do not require a license.

CB radios: Citizens Band (CB) radios are popular for their long-range capabilities and ease of use. They can be installed in vehicles or used as base stations in homes. CB radios have a range of up to 30 miles, depending on antenna type and installation. No license is required to operate a CB radio.

FRS/GMRS radios: Family Radio Service (FRS) and General Mobile Radio Service (GMRS) radios are similar to walkie-talkies but offer increased power and range. FRS radios have a range of up to 2 miles, while GMRS radios can communicate up to 25 miles or more. A license is required for GMRS radios, but not for

FRS radios.

HAM radios: Amateur (HAM) radios offer the greatest range and versatility of all two-way radio options. They can communicate over hundreds or even thousands of miles, depending on equipment and conditions. HAM radio operators require a license from the Federal Communications Commission (FCC) and must pass an exam to demonstrate knowledge of radio theory, regulations, and operating practices.

Range, power, and frequency considerations

When choosing a two-way radio, consider the range, power, and frequency options that best suit your needs. Range can be affected by terrain, obstructions, and atmospheric conditions. Higher-powered radios generally offer longer range, but also consume more battery power. Keep in mind that radios with removable antennas can often be upgraded with aftermarket antennas for increased range. Keep the following factors in mind to make an informed decision:

Range: Assess your communication requirements based on your location and the distance you need to cover. In urban areas or places with dense vegetation, signal strength can be significantly reduced. If you live in a rural or remote area, a radio with a longer range is essential. It's also important to remember that manufacturers often overstate the range of their devices under optimal conditions. Therefore, it's wise to choose a radio with a range greater than your actual needs.

Power output: The power output of a radio affects its range and battery consumption. Higher power output generally increases range, but it also drains the battery faster. Consider a radio with adjustable power output so you can balance range and battery life according to your needs.

Frequencies and bands: Two-way radios operate on different frequency bands, such as VHF (Very High Frequency) and UHF (Ultra High Frequency). VHF radios work best in open areas and over long distances with minimal obstructions, while UHF radios are better suited for urban environments or situations with more obstacles. Some radios offer dual-band capabilities, allowing you to switch between VHF and UHF as needed.

Channels and privacy codes: The number of available channels and privacy codes can influence your communication options. More channels provide greater flexibility in finding a clear frequency, while privacy codes help minimize interference from other users. Look for a radio with adequate channel and privacy code options for your anticipated needs.

Antennas: The type and quality of the antenna can greatly impact the range and performance of your radio. Radios with removable antennas offer the advantage of upgrading to aftermarket antennas for improved range and signal clarity. Consider investing in a high-quality antenna to maximize your radio's capabilities.

Weather resistance and durability: You may need to use your radio outdoors or in harsh conditions. Choose a radio that is built to withstand the elements and is constructed with durable materials.

Ease of use: During an emergency, it's crucial to have a radio that is easy to operate. Look for radios with user-friendly controls, clear displays, and intuitive menu systems. Additionally, consider purchasing a radio with a backlit display for improved visibility in low-light conditions.

Remember to test your radio regularly and familiarize yourself with its operation to ensure you are ready to communicate effectively when the need arises.

Licensing requirements and operating guidelines

While some two-way radio services, such as FRS and CB, do not require a license, others, like GMRS and HAM radios, do. To obtain a GMRS license, you must apply through the FCC and pay a fee. For HAM radio, you need to pass an examination to demonstrate your knowledge of radio theory, regulations, and operating practices. Make sure you understand the licensing requirements for your chosen radio service and follow all applicable operating guidelines.

Tips for effective radio communication

Learn radio etiquette: Familiarize yourself with common radio phrases and procedures to ensure clear and efficient communication.

Use the right channel: Choose a channel that is not in use or has minimal interference to avoid cross-talk with other users.

Speak clearly and concisely: Articulate your words, speak slowly, and keep your message brief to ensure it is understood.

Confirm receipt of messages: Ask the recipient to acknowledge receipt of your message to ensure it has been received and understood.

Monitor battery life: Keep an eye on your radio's battery level and have spare batteries or a charging solution on hand.

Regularly test your equipment: Periodically test your radios to ensure they are functioning properly and that you are familiar with their operation.

Emergency Alert Systems (EAS)

During a blackout, staying informed about ongoing emergencies, potential threats, and safety instructions is crucial. Emergency alert systems (EAS) are designed to provide the public with important updates about imminent threats or ongoing emergencies, such as natural disasters, hazardous material spills, or terrorist attacks. The primary goal of these systems is to save lives and protect property by providing actionable information that helps individuals to make informed decisions during a crisis. In this section, we will discuss the different types of EAS and how you can prepare your home to receive these alerts.

Types of EAS: weather radios, television, and internet-based alerts

There are several types of emergency alert systems that can be used, each with its advantages and limitations.

Weather radios: NOAA (National Oceanic and Atmospheric Administration) Weather Radio All Hazards (NWR) is a nationwide network of radio stations that broadcast weather and emergency information. These radios are specifically designed to receive alerts from the NOAA, and they can operate on battery or hand-crank power sources. Weather radios provide real-time updates on severe weather events and other hazards, making them a valuable tool for emergency preparedness.

Television: Local television stations often broadcast emergency alerts and provide essential information about ongoing crises. However, relying on television broadcasts during a blackout can be problematic, as it requires access to a functioning television and a power source.

Internet-based alerts: Various online platforms and apps provide emergency alerts, including the Wireless Emergency Alerts (WEA) system, which sends text messages to compatible mobile devices in the event of an emergency. However, internet-based alerts are dependent on the availability of internet access and cellular networks, which may be disrupted when the grid goes down.

Preparing your home with EAS equipment

To stay connected and informed during a grid-down event, it's essential to prepare your home with appropriate EAS equipment. Here are some steps you can take:

Purchase a weather radio: Invest in a reliable weather radio with battery or hand-crank power options. Place the radio in a central location within your home, and familiarize yourself with its operation.

Consider a battery-powered television: While not as portable as a weather radio, having a battery-powered television can provide additional information during an emergency. Be aware that television signals may be disrupted or unavailable during a power outage.

Keep backup power sources: Have backup power sources available for your EAS equipment, such as extra batteries or solar chargers. Ensure that these power sources are maintained and readily accessible.

Test your EAS equipment regularly: Regularly test your emergency alert systems to ensure they are functioning correctly and that you are familiar with their operation.

By incorporating EAS equipment into your preparedness plan, you can make informed decisions during emergency.

Connecting with Local Community Groups and Networks

In addition to monitoring news broadcasts and emergency alerts, connecting with local community groups and networks can provide valuable support during a power outage. These groups can include neighborhood associations, emergency preparedness groups, amateur radio clubs, and volunteer organizations such as the Community Emergency Response Team (CERT).

By joining local community groups, you can build a network of people who can share updates and tips. This network can help you stay informed about local conditions and provide updates on available resources, such as shelters, food distribution points, and medical services. Additionally, by collaborating with your community, you can pool resources and knowledge, increasing your collective resilience when the grid goes down.

In conclusion, staying informed during a grid-down event is critical for making decisions about your safety. By utilizing alternative communication methods such as battery-powered or hand-crank radios and connecting with local community groups, you can increase your ability to stay informed and face the challenges.

Key Takeaways

In this chapter, we have explored various communication and connectivity strategies to stay connected. The key takeaways include:

Landline phones offer a reliable communication option, as they are less susceptible to infrastructure failures compared to cell phones.

Cell phones and mobile networks can still be utilized, but battery conservation and portable charging options should be considered.

Two-way radios, including walkie-talkies, CB radios, FRS/GMRS radios, and HAM radios, provide alternative communication methods with varying ranges, power, and frequencies.

Emergency Alert Systems (EAS) can help you stay informed about ongoing emergencies and receive crucial updates through weather radios, television, and internet-based alerts.

Staying informed during a grid-down situation can be achieved by monitoring news and updates, utilizing battery-powered or hand-crank AM/FM radios, and connecting with local community groups and networks.

In the next chapter, we will discuss how to keep your home safe and secure during a power outage. We will explore various strategies, such as reinforcing doors and windows, establishing a secure perimeter, and focusing on personal safety and self-defense, to ensure your family's safety during times of crisis.

CHAPTER NINE

HOME SECURITY AND PROTECTION

The ultimate aim of martial arts is not
having to use them.

Miyamoto Musashi

An extended power outage can lead to increased crime rates, as streets are dark, security systems are down, and law enforcement resources are stretched thin. In these challenging circumstances, fortifying your home is a necessity to protect your family and property from opportunistic criminals.

In this chapter, we'll walk you through the steps you need to take to transform your home into a secure fortress. Together, we'll explore home fortification, and by the end of this chapter, your house will be well-prepared to face the challenges.

Assessing Security Vulnerabilities

Before you can effectively fortify your home, it's essential to assess its current security vulnerabilities. This process will help you identify weak spots and prioritize improvements to create a safe and secure environment.

Identifying potential entry points

Begin by walking around your property and identifying all potential entry points. This includes doors, windows, and other access points such as basement windows, garage doors, and pet doors. Be thorough in your assessment and think like an intruder—what points of entry might they exploit to gain access to your home?

Evaluating the strength of doors and windows

Once you've identified all potential entry points, evaluate the strength of your doors and windows. Are your doors solid and sturdy, or could they be easily kicked in? Do your windows have secure locks or are they easily opened from the outside? Pay special attention to sliding glass doors and ground-level windows, as these are often targeted by burglars.

Assessing the visibility of your property

Another crucial factor in home security is the visibility of your property. Are there areas where intruders could hide, such as tall shrubs or poorly-lit corners? Are valuable items visible from the street, potentially attracting thieves? Assess the visibility of your property from both the outside and the inside, considering how you could improve your line of sight to deter potential intruders.

Checking the effectiveness of your existing security measures

Finally, review your existing security measures and determine their effectiveness in a power outage scenario. Do you have security cameras, motion detectors, or alarm systems that rely on electricity? Will these systems still function during a blackout, or do you need to invest in alternative, off-grid security measures?

By assessing your home's security weak points, you can create a plan to address these issues. In the following sections, we'll explore strategies to fortify your home.

Reinforcing Doors and Windows

In a grid-down situation, ensuring that your home's doors and windows are secure becomes even more critical. Taking steps to reinforce these potential entry points can greatly reduce the risk of unwanted intruders entering your home.

Upgrading door locks and deadbolts

One of the first steps in reinforcing your doors is to upgrade the locks and deadbolts. Look for high-quality locks with a proven track record of resisting forced entry, such as ANSI Grade 1 deadbolts. Consider adding additional deadbolts to your doors for an extra layer of security. For added protection, install a door chain or latch, which can help prevent intruders from gaining full access even if they manage to unlock the door.

Implementing door reinforcement kits

Another way to bolster your home's security is by installing door reinforcement kits. These kits typically include a combination of metal plates, brackets, and hardware designed to reinforce the doorjamb, lock, and hinges. By strengthening these weak points, you can make it much more difficult for intruders to kick in your door or force their way inside. Be sure to choose a kit that is compatible with your specific door type and follow the manufacturer's installation instructions carefully.

Adding window film for shatter resistance

Intruders may attempt to gain entry by breaking windows, which can be especially concerning during a power outage when help may be delayed. Adding shatter-resistant window film to your windows can help prevent glass from breaking or, at the very least, make it more difficult for intruders to get through. This film also offers the added benefit of reducing heat transfer and UV exposure, improving your home's overall energy efficiency.

By taking these steps to reinforce doors and windows, you can improve your home's security during a power outage.

Perimeter Security and Surveillance

Perimeter security means setting up defenses around the outer edge of your property to keep intruders out. By establishing a strong perimeter, installing appropriate lighting, utilizing alternative surveillance methods, and creating natural barriers, you can deter intruders and maintain your home's security even without electricity.

Establishing a secure perimeter

Establishing a secure perimeter involves controlling access to your property and making it more challenging for intruders to approach your home unnoticed. Start by ensuring that fences and gates are in good condition and securely locked. Clear away any debris, tall grass, or overgrown vegetation that could provide cover for intruders. Additionally, consider installing signage warning of the presence of security measures, even if they are not functional during the power outage. This can serve as a psychological deterrent for would-be intruders.

Installing motion-activated lights

Although electricity may not be available during a power outage, you can still utilize motion-activated lights that are solar-powered or battery-operated. These lights can help illuminate your property when movement is detected, making it more difficult for intruders to approach without being noticed. Place these lights strategically around your property, focusing on entry points and areas with limited visibility.

Utilizing security cameras and alternative surveillance methods

In the absence of electricity, traditional security cameras may not be functional. However, you can use battery-operated or solar-powered cameras as an alternative. Additionally, consider using dummy cameras as a deterrent. They can give the appearance of surveillance without actually recording footage.

Another alternative surveillance method is to establish a neighborhood watch system. Work with your neighbors to create a network of individuals who are committed to monitoring and reporting any suspicious activity in the area.

Creating natural barriers and deterrents

Natural barriers can serve as effective deterrents to intruders. Planting thorny bushes or installing gravel walkways can create obstacles and noise, making it more difficult for intruders to approach your home undetected. Additionally, strategically placed landscaping features, such as large rocks or raised flower beds, can help impede access to your property.

By implementing these perimeter security and surveillance measures, you can help protect your home and loved ones during a power outage. These strategies can not only enhance your home's security but also provide peace of mind in the face of potential threats.

Personal Safety and Self-Defense

When faced with a power outage, ensuring personal safety and self-defense becomes a top priority. In such situations, it's crucial to be well-versed in the self-defense tools and techniques available to you, as well as the establishment of safe rooms and escape routes within your home.

Self-defense tools and techniques

Self-defense classes can provide practical skills to help you protect yourself and your family in dangerous situations. Martial arts courses, such as karate or Brazilian jiu-jitsu, can also provide valuable training in self-defense.

In addition to self-defense training, it's essential to have access to reliable tools. Pepper spray, stun guns, and personal alarms are common examples of self-defense devices that can be employed during an emergency. Be sure to research local laws and regulations on the possession and use of such tools, as restrictions may apply in some areas.

Safe rooms and escape routes

Designating safe rooms and escape routes in your home can provide an added layer of security. A safe room is a specific area where you and your family can retreat quickly and securely in case of an emergency. Ideally, this room should be reinforced to withstand potential threats and stocked with essential supplies, such as food, water, first aid kits, and self-defense tools.

Multiple escape routes should also be identified throughout your home, offering various exit points in case one route becomes inaccessible. Practice using these escape routes with your family, ensuring that everyone is familiar with the best ways to leave the house safely if necessary. It's crucial to keep these routes unobstructed and to have a plan for how to navigate them in low-light conditions during a power outage.

Key Takeaways

In this chapter, we have discussed various aspects of fortifying your home and ensuring your family's safety during a power outage. Here are the key takeaways from this chapter:

Assessing your home's security vulnerabilities by identifying potential entry points, evaluating the strength of doors and windows, assessing property visibility, and checking the effectiveness of existing security measures.

Reinforcing doors and windows with upgraded door locks and deadbolts, adding window film for shatter resistance, and implementing door reinforcement kits.

Establishing a secure perimeter, installing motion-activated lights, utilizing security cameras and alternative surveillance methods, and creating natural barriers and deterrents for perimeter security and surveillance.

Focusing on personal safety and self-defense, including learning self-defense techniques, acquiring suitable self-defense tools, designating safe rooms, and establishing escape routes in your home.

Chapter Ten

THRIVING IN LONG-TERM POWER OUTAGE

It is not the strongest of the species that
survives, nor the most intelligent; it is the
one most responsive to change.

Charles Darwin

The idea of a long-term grid down scenario might seem far-fetched, but as the world becomes increasingly unpredictable due to factors such as climate change, economic instability, and political unrest, the possibility of power outages lasting months or even years is not entirely out of the question. In fact, David Crawford's novel "Lights Out" provides an insightful and captivating portrayal of what life could look like under such circumstances. The story follows a tight-knit community as they navigate the challenges of a sudden, widespread and prolonged power outage and the ensuing chaos from an EMP attack. The novel emphasizes the importance of preparedness, adaptability, and community resilience, offering valuable lessons on the skills and mindset necessary to survive and thrive.

In this chapter, we will discuss the strategies and mindset necessary to not only survive, but also thrive during a prolonged power outage. We will explore how to overcome the challenges that arise, adapt to a new way of living.

Overcoming Prolonged Challenges

In a prolonged power outage, challenges can arise that may greatly impact your daily life. Overcoming these challenges requires a combination of resourcefulness, self-sufficiency, and strong community support.

One common challenge is the lack of access to essential resources such as food, water, and medical supplies. To address this issue, it's important to build up a stockpile of non-perishable food items, water purification supplies, and necessary medications well in advance. Keep your emergency supplies fresh and ready by regularly checking and rotating them.

Another challenge is the absence of conventional heating and cooling systems, which can make it difficult to maintain a comfortable indoor environment. To counter this, consider incorporating passive heating and cooling techniques into your home design or retrofitting your existing home with energy-efficient measures. Using different ways to heat and cool your place, like wood stoves for warmth and smart shading for cooling, can really make your home more comfortable.

Building self-sufficiency and autonomy involves learning new skills and becoming less reliant on external systems. This can include growing your own food and learning how to repair and maintain essential equipment. By developing a diverse set of skills and knowledge, you'll be better equipped to tackle the challenges that may arise.

It's also crucial to recognize the importance of communication. Staying informed about the ongoing situation and connecting with others is vital for both practical and emotional support. Establishing communication methods, such as two-way radios or satellite phones, can help you maintain contact with your network and gather important information.

Developing a support network is another key aspect. This network can consist of friends, family, and neighbors who can provide help and resources when needed. Strengthening these connections by regularly engaging with your community and participating in local initiatives can be invaluable during a crisis. In turn, you can offer your own skills and resources to support others in need.

Adapting to a New Way of Life

In the event of a long-term grid down scenario, adapting to a new way of life becomes essential for survival. This may involve learning new skills and trades, embracing alternative energy sources and sustainable living practices, as well as establishing new routines and habits.

Learning new skills and trades

To become self-sufficient and better equipped to handle the challenges, it's crucial to acquire new skills and trades. These may include gardening, woodworking, sewing, first aid, and basic electrical and plumbing repairs. By learning these skills, you not only increase your chances of survival but also enhance your ability to contribute to the well-being of your community.

Furthermore, having a wide range of skills can help you barter for goods and services when traditional currency systems are disrupted.

Establishing new routines and habits

Adapting to a new way of life also entails establishing new routines and habits to cope with the changing circumstances. This may involve adjusting your sleep schedule to align with natural daylight hours, creating a daily task list to maintain productivity, and developing an exercise routine to stay physically fit.

Adapting to a new way of life during a long-term grid down scenario requires a combination of learning new skills and establishing routines that promote physical and emotional well-being. By taking these steps, you can ensure your survival and create a more resilient and self-sufficient lifestyle.

Building Resilient Communities

Building resilient communities involves fostering strong support networks, collaborating with neighbors and organizations, and enhancing local preparedness initiatives. By taking collective action, communities can effectively address the challenges and become more self-sufficient in the process.

The Strength of Support Networks

One of the most important aspects of community resilience is the establishment of robust support networks. These networks can provide emotional, logistical, and resource assistance during challenging times.

Support networks can take many forms, including family members, friends, neighbors, and even local organizations. By actively engaging with those around you and forming bonds based on trust and cooperation, you can create a reliable network that will help you navigate the difficulties. These connections can offer invaluable support in the form of shared resources, skills, and knowledge. Regular communication, collaboration, and mutual assistance are the cornerstones of a strong support network.

Collaborating with Neighbors and Organizations

Working together with neighbors and local organizations can significantly improve the overall resilience of a community. By pooling resources, sharing skills, and coordinating efforts, communities can address various challenges more efficiently and effectively.

Start conversations with your neighbors about their preparedness plans and discuss how you might support one another during a crisis. Identify local organizations, such as churches, schools, or community centers, that serve as hubs for information and resources. Engage with these organizations to discuss preparedness plans and identify potential areas of collaboration.

Additionally, consider participating in or organizing community preparedness events, such as training sessions, workshops, or disaster drills. These events can provide opportunities for community members to learn new skills, share valuable knowledge, and strengthen their support networks.

Building resilient communities is an essential aspect of overall preparedness. By fostering strong support networks, collaborating with neighbors and organizations, and enhancing local preparedness initiatives, communities can effectively tackle the challenges posed by prolonged power outages.

Key Takeaways

In this chapter, we have discussed various aspects of thriving in long-term grid down scenarios. The most important points include:

Overcoming prolonged power outage challenges by identifying common difficulties and finding solutions, building self-sufficiency, and developing a support network. This entails addressing both physical and logistical challenges while also focusing on mental and emotional well-being.

Establish new routines and habits that align with the realities of a grid down scenario, helping to ease the transition and maintain a sense of normalcy.

Robust support networks are crucial for community resilience. Engaging with family, friends, neighbors, and local organizations creates a web of support. This network becomes a foundation for sharing resources, skills, and knowledge, vital for navigating challenging times.

Proactively identifying and contributing to local preparedness initiatives is key. This involves joining or establishing neighborhood programs, community gardens, or emergency response teams. Filling gaps in community preparedness by leading new projects ensures a well-rounded approach to tackling challenges.

By taking these steps, you can successfully navigate the hardships of long-term grid down scenarios, emerging stronger and more self-sufficient.

In the next chapter, we will explore the financial aspects of grid down preparedness. We will cover topics such as building an emergency fund, diversifying income sources, and safeguarding important financial documents. The knowledge will help you establish a solid financial foundation to face the challenges.

Chapter Eleven

FINANCIAL PREPAREDNESS

An emergency fund turns a crisis into an
inconvenience.

Dave Ramsey

The importance of financial preparedness cannot be overstated. As we have seen in previous chapters, power outages can impact various aspects of our lives, from basic needs like food and water to communication and safety. However, one area that is often overlooked is the financial aspect of living through an extended power outage.

During a power outage, access to banks, ATMs, and electronic payment systems may be severely disrupted, making it difficult to access your funds or make transactions. Moreover, prolonged power outages can lead to job losses, business closures, and other economic disruptions that can significantly impact your financial stability. Additionally, the cost of emergency supplies, alternative energy sources, and other necessary items can quickly add up, straining your budget.

In this chapter, we will explore various strategies to ensure that you are financially prepared. We will discuss the importance of having an emergency fund, diversifying your assets, and planning for the potential economic fallout. By taking the steps outlined in this chapter, you can better safeguard your financial well-being.

Creating an Emergency Fund

An emergency fund plays an important role, it provides financial security and stability when income sources may become uncertain or disrupted. Having a financial safety net ensures that you can take care of your loved ones without resorting to desperate measures or falling into debt.

Determining how much money to set aside for emergencies depends on your personal needs, such as your family size, living expenses, and risk factors. A general rule of thumb is to have a minimum of three to six months' worth of living expenses set aside for emergencies.

Building an emergency fund seems daunting, especially if you are starting from scratch. Here are some tips to help you create a robust financial buffer:

Set a realistic goal: Determine the target amount for the emergency fund based on your unique circumstances.

Budget for savings: Include your emergency fund as a line item in your monthly budget, treating it as a non-negotiable expense. Prioritize savings over spending.

Automate savings: Set up a scheduled transfer from your checking account to a savings account each month to automate your savings process. This eliminates the need for manual transfers and ensures consistent progress toward your goal.

Cut expenses: Look for areas where you can cut back or eliminate expenses. Reducing spending, such as dining out, entertainment, or shopping, can free up funds to allocate toward your emergency savings.

Increase your income: Consider taking on a side job, freelancing, or selling items you no longer need to supplement your income. Direct any additional earnings toward your emergency fund.

Save windfalls: Whenever you receive unexpected money, such as a bonus, tax refund, or gift, consider putting all or a portion of it into your emergency fund.

Diversifying Your Assets

By spreading your resources across various forms of currency and investments, you can reduce risk and maintain access to funds even when traditional financial systems may be compromised. Here, we explore some alternative forms of currency and the role they can play in grid-down preparedness.

Cash: Cash is an accepted form of currency for purchasing essential goods and services. It is crucial to have an adequate supply of cash stored securely at home, in various denominations, to facilitate transactions when electronic payment methods may not be operational.

Precious metals: Gold and silver are a reliable store of value and can serve as an alternative currency during times of crisis. These tangible assets are relatively immune to inflation and can be easily traded or bartered when necessary. Investing in small denominations of gold and silver coins or bars can provide a hedge against currency devaluation and ensure that you have a means of exchange.

Cryptocurrency: While cryptocurrencies such as Bitcoin rely on internet access and functioning power grids for transactions, they may still have a role to play in long-term preparedness. As decentralized digital assets, cryptocurrencies can be resistant to government intervention or financial institution collapse. In a prolonged crisis or a situation where traditional currency becomes unstable, cryptocurrencies may offer an alternative means of exchange.

Bartering: Bartering involves exchanging goods or services directly, without the need for a common currency. This age-old practice can be invaluable where access to traditional currency becomes unreliable. Stockpiling items of value for bartering, such as non-perishable food, tools, or medical supplies, can provide a means of obtaining essential goods and services. Additionally, developing valuable skills like carpentry, gardening, or first aid can also serve as barterable assets in times of crisis.

Maintaining Essential Insurance Policies

Insurance offers a safety net to protect your financial stability and help you recover from unforeseen events that may occur during a crisis. As part of your financial preparedness plan, it is essential to maintain adequate insurance coverage for your home, property, and belongings, as well as review and update your policies regularly.

Insurance can provide financial support to help you rebuild and recover from damages caused by events such as natural disasters, theft, or other emergencies. For instance, if a storm damages your home during a prolonged power outage, having the right insurance policy in place can provide the funds needed to repair the damage and replace lost or damaged belongings.

To ensure adequate coverage, it is crucial to assess your home, property, and personal belongings' value and determine the risks you may face in your area. This assessment should include considering potential natural disasters, such as floods, hurricanes, or earthquakes, and understanding how your insurance policies protect against these hazards. It is also essential to be aware of any coverage limits or exclusions of your policies.

Managing Debt and Expenses

Developing strategies for reducing and managing debt, as well as controlling expenses, can help you maintain financial stability.

Make a list of all your debts, such as credit cards, loans, and any other debts you owe. Prioritize these debts based on interest rates and repayment terms, focusing on paying off high-interest debts first. If possible, consolidate debts into a single loan with a reduced interest rate to simplify your payments and lower the overall cost.

Controlling expenses involves reevaluating your spending habits and prioritizing essential needs. Create a budget that focuses on necessities such as food, water, shelter, and medical supplies while cutting back on non-essential spending. Look for ways to reduce costs, such as growing your own food, or utilizing energy-efficient appliances. It is also important to avoid making impulsive purchases that can strain your financial resources.

Key Takeaways

In this chapter, we have discussed the importance of financial preparedness. The key takeaways include:

Creating an emergency fund: An emergency fund plays a major role in providing financial security during a grid-down situation. Set aside enough money to cover several months' worth of living expenses and work towards building your fund gradually.

Diversifying your assets: Consider alternative forms of currency, such as cash, precious metals, cryptocurrency, and bartering, to ensure you have access to resources.

Maintaining essential insurance policies: Ensure adequate coverage for your home, property, and belongings, and review and update insurance policies regularly to reflect your current needs and circumstances.

Managing debt and expenses: Develop strategies for reducing and managing debt, and control expenses by prioritizing essential needs and creating a budget tailored for emergency situations.

CHAPTER TWELVE

YOUR GRID DOWN PREPAREDNESS JOURNEY

Well, it's been quite the adventure as we've delved into the world of grid-down preparedness. We've explored the ins and outs of surviving and thriving during power outages, whether they're short-term or here for the long haul.

We know what you're thinking – "Phew, that was a lot of information!" And you're right, it is. But don't worry, preparedness is not a one-size-fits-all adventure. It's a journey that you can tailor to your unique needs and situations.

First things first, it's important to remember that Rome wasn't built in a day, and neither will your emergency preparedness plan. It's a marathon, not a sprint. Start by prioritizing the most critical aspects of your plan, such as securing water, food, and shelter. Once you've got the basics covered, you can begin working on the more advanced things.

Remember, preparedness is not an all-or-nothing game. Every little step you take, no matter how small, is progress. So, don't feel overwhelmed by the magnitude of the task at hand. Instead, break it down into smaller tasks, and celebrate each victory as you complete them.

Next, let's talk about the power of community. You're not in this alone. Chances are, your friends, family, and neighbors are just as concerned about getting prepared as you are. Reach out to them, share your knowledge, and learn from one another. You might even inspire them to join you on this exciting journey. Together, you can build a strong support network that will make any emergency a little less daunting.

Now, let's address the elephant in the room: the dreaded "P" word – procrastination. We've all been there, telling ourselves we'll start preparing "tomorrow," only to find that tomorrow never comes. Well, the time for action is now. Don't let the fear of the unknown or the sheer volume of tasks paralyze you. Instead, remind yourself of the wise words of Karen Lamb: "A year from now, you'll wish you had started today."

Lastly, don't forget to enjoy the process. Preparedness may seem like a serious and daunting subject, but it can also be a fun and rewarding journey. Embrace the opportunity to learn new skills, meet like-minded people, and become more self-reliant. You'll be amazed at how empowering it can be to know that you're capable of facing adversity head-on.

As we end this book, remember that the journey is as important as the destination. Start where you are, use what you have, and do what you can. The efforts you make today will help ensure that if the lights go out, you're not left in the dark. Embrace the challenge and continue to build your preparedness, step by step.

SHARE YOUR THOUGHTS

As you come to the end of this book, we hope it has offered you information and strategies for ensuring your safety and well-being when the grid goes down, and we would be honored to hear your thoughts.

Please consider leave an honest review on Amazon. Your feedback is not only crucial to us but also to other readers interested in a self-sufficient lifestyle. Whether it's an insight you found useful, a story you'd like to share, or suggestions for future editions, your voice matters.

Thank you for choosing this guide, and for taking the time to help us improve. Your support is greatly appreciated!

RESOURCES

You've made it to the end of this book, but your journey to grid-down preparedness is far from over. Here are some fantastic resources to help you continue your learning journey.

Books

Here are some classic books on preparedness and self-sufficiency that have been popular and well-regarded:

- "When Technology Fails" by Matthew Stein – An excellent resource for anyone looking to build resilience and adapt to life without modern conveniences.

- "The Prepper's Blueprint" by Tess Pennington – A practical guide to help you plan and prepare for various disaster scenarios.

- "The SAS Survival Handbook" by John 'Lofty' Wiseman – Written by a former SAS soldier, this book covers essential survival skills and techniques, making it a valuable resource for anyone interested in preparedness.

- "The Prepper's Pocket Guide" by Bernie Carr – This book offers practical tips and advice for preparing your home and family for various types of disasters, from natural disasters to economic collapse.

- "The Survival Medicine Handbook" by Joseph Alton MD and Amy Alton ARNP – This book focuses on medical preparedness and provides guidance on handling various medical emergencies when professional help is not available.

Authority Websites

Government and organizational websites can offer reliable information and resources to help you with your preparedness journey. Some noteworthy websites include:

- Ready.gov (www.ready.gov) – The official emergency preparedness website of the U.S. Department of Homeland Security, offering a wealth of information on how to prepare for and respond to various types of disasters.

- The American Red Cross (www.redcross.org) – This organization provides a range of resources related to disaster preparedness, including tips, checklists, and online training courses.

- The National Center for Disaster Preparedness (ncdp.columbia.edu) – A research center at Columbia University that offers resources and information on disaster preparedness, response, and recovery.

Local and Social Media Groups

Connecting with like-minded people can be a valuable source of support, advice, and inspiration. Look for local preparedness groups in your area by searching on social media sites like Facebook or Meetup. You can also join online communities to learn from others around the world. Some popular social media groups include:

- American Preppers Network (www.facebook.com/AmericanPreppersNetwork) – A Facebook group dedicated to promoting preparedness through information sharing and networking.

• Off-Grid Living & Homesteading (www.facebook.com/ groups/offgridlivingandhomesteading) – This Facebook group provides a platform for off-grid enthusiasts to share experiences, tips, and advice on living a self-sufficient life-style.

• The Preparedness Subreddit (www.reddit.com/r/preppers) – A Reddit community where preppers can discuss and share information related to emergency preparedness, survivalism, and self-sufficiency.

YouTube Channels

YouTube is a fantastic place for learning new skills, and there are numerous channels dedicated to preparedness and off-grid living. Here are a few popular channels to check out:

• City Prepping (www.youtube.com/c/CityPrepping) – This channel focuses on urban preparedness, offering practical tips and advice for city dwellers looking to become more self-reliant.

• Canadian Prepper (www.youtube.com/c/CanadianPrep-per) - A comprehensive channel covering survival, emergency preparedness, gear reviews, and prepping strategies with a focus on both urban and wilderness settings.

• Survival Dispatch (www.youtube.com/c/SurvivalDis-patch) - A resource for survival and preparedness education, featuring expert interviews, gear reviews, and survival tips for a variety of scenarios.

- The Patriot Nurse (www.youtube.com/user/ThePatriot-Nurse) - This channel focuses on medical preparedness and healthcare strategies, combining general survival advice with in-depth medical knowledge.

By tapping into these resources, you can further develop your skills, knowledge, and connections within the preparedness and off-grid living communities. Continue to learn and grow, and you'll be better equipped to face any grid-down situation with confidence and resilience.

www.ingramcontent.com/pod-product-compliance
Lightning Source LLC
Chambersburg PA
CBHW030920140626
46545CB00016B/2272